Dedication

I would like to dedicate this book to my late husband, George, in memory of the deep bond of love which united us throughout our long life's journey, from the terrors of Nazi Germany to the founding of Roeper City and Country School in Michigan, and to our retirement in California. He was a peaceful man whose presence gave many, many people the courage to be themselves.

Acknowledgments

This book represents the essence of an important aspect of my life. Roeper City and Country School is where my husband George and I implemented our philosophy. My writings and speeches are where I expressed my thoughts and dreams.

By publishing this volume, Judy Galbraith afforded me the opportunity of creating an overview of my ideas and presenting them as an organic whole. Her co-worker, Pamela Espeland, and R.C. Medeiros edited the greater number of the articles, working hard to create a unifying structure to organize my work. I am grateful to them for their assistance. The rest of the editing was done by my dear friend, Linda Silverman, whose personal empathy with me and my work allowed her to highlight my ideas through her carefully thought-out finishing touches. Many heartfelt thanks go to her. I also want to thank Constance Shannon, who put the original collection together, Anne Beneventi, who helped me in more ways than I can describe, and Judy Wendell, who searched for many of the lost references and helped in many other ways.

Since I lost all my manuscripts when our house burned in the Oakland fire, this book could not exist if it had not been for the many, many dear friends from all over the world who found copies of my articles and sent them to me. Many thanks to all of them.

ANNEMARIE ROEPER

Selected Writings and Speeches

Annemarie Roeper, Ed.D.

free Spirit
PUBLISHING

Library of Congress Cataloging-in-Publication Data
Roeper, Annemarie, 1918–
   [Selections. 1995]
   Annemarie Roeper : selected writings and speeches / Annemarie
Roeper : foreword by Linda Kreger Silverman.
       p.   cm.
   Includes bibliographical references and index.
   ISBN 0-915793-93-8 (alk. paper)
   1. Gifted children—Education—United States—Philosophy.
2. Gifted children—United States—Psychology. 3. Parenting—United
States. I. Title.
LC3993.9.R64 1995
371.95'0973—dc20   95-19340
                                                                           CIP

Edited by R.C. Medeiros, Linda Kreger Silverman, and Pamela Espcland
Cover and book design by MacLean & Tuminelly
Index prepared by Eileen Quam and Theresa Wolner
10 9 8 7 6 5 4 3 2 1
Printed in the United States of America

Free Spirit Publishing Inc.
400 First Avenue North, Suite 616
Minneapolis, MN 55401-1730
(612) 338-2068

Contents

Foreword

I am deeply honored to be asked to write a foreword to this compilation of Annemarie Roeper's work. Annemarie's voice is the small whisper of conscience we can hear whenever we quiet our busy minds enough to hear the truth. It is perfect that this collection of articles begins with "Truth and the Young Child." In 1939, Leta Hollingworth wrote, "...in the end the truth will be admitted and utilized, as everything is finally utilized that has power to bring order to human life" (p. 579). Had she lived to read this collection, I'm sure Leta would concur that in these pages Annemarie has shared profound truths that have the "power to bring order to human life." This book will not appeal to those who are insincere or unscrupulous. The first of these articles bears witness to Annemarie's exquisite moral sensitivity. Despite the many years that we have been friends, I was awestruck by the penetrating insights in this article, one of which is captured in the quotation that commences the anthology:

> "The result...is almost a conspiracy of silence which is reciprocated by children. It is as though a mutual agreement exists that certain things, even though obvious to all, simply have not occurred. This means that we may believe we have succeeded in keeping certain realities from children, while, in actuality, they have successfully kept their concerns from us. The consequence is that they are forced to deal with difficult problems by themselves and are left to face questions without help, for which they are neither emotionally nor intellectually equipped."

And that's only the beginning: The entire collection is filled with pearls you will cherish, reread, and share with others for the rest of your life. Annemarie's book was not meant to grace your coffee table or adorn your bookshelf; you will turn to it again and again for guidance. Just glance through the quotations that launch each article for a glimpse of what awaits you. In your hands is a treasure that will delight and deepen you, disturb and comfort you, enlighten and inspire you. Be prepared to buy a lending copy!

In the tradition of Leta Hollingworth—the foremother and matron saint of our field—Annemarie brings us far-reaching vision and deep, heartfelt wisdom. And, like Leta, Annemarie has the uncanny ability to get inside the heart and soul of the gifted child; these children trust her implicitly. Annemarie brings you this "view from the inside out" that she has gleaned throughout her career from listening patiently to the deepest thoughts of hundreds of gifted children. Her abiding respect for children permeates every page.

There is something for everyone in this book because Annemarie brings the perspective of so many different roles to her writing. She has been a nursery school teacher, an administrator, a psychoanalytically trained therapist, an organizer, a parent and parent advocate, a parenting columnist, a consultant to parents and schools, a speaker, a researcher, and a prolific writer. Most of all, she is a philosopher. Her philosophy of self-actualization and interdependence is beautiful, simple, and accessible to everyone. It illuminates all of her writing.

Annemarie lives her philosophy. She is one of the few evolved souls on the planet for whom ends never justify means. (See "The Global Perspective.") While a strong supporter of causes, her way is gentle— totally nonviolent. In these pages, you will see the power of her metaphors, examples, and reasoning. Many of these articles were written originally as speeches, and her words communicate directly to your soul. You may find yourself changed as a result of reading this compilation: more committed to making a difference with your life.

In "How Gifted Children Cope with Their Emotions," Annemarie introduced gifted education to the concept of emotional giftedness (Piechowski, 1991). This is a classic in the field that has clearly influenced state-of-the-art thinking about the emotional facets of giftedness. Her insights about the unique development of gifted children—their combination of unusual awareness, emotional sensitivity, and uneven development which leads to an inability to fit in—inspired a new conception of giftedness as *asynchronous development* (Columbus Group, 1991).

Her article, "Parenting the Gifted," delineates these developmental differences:

> "Gifted children have a tendency to surprise us with their advanced abilities, their knowledge, their ability to generalize, their sensitivity, their astute observations, their mature logic, their insights, their unusual interests, their incredible memories, and so forth. On the other hand, they often appear infantile,

they may be argumentative, and they have a tendency to be loners. Many seem to be unable to fit into a regular classroom."

In the same article, Annemarie describes innate characteristics she has observed in gifted infants:

"Gifted children are different from the day they are born; they don't become different all of a sudden. Newborn babies have an awareness, a liveliness, and, sometimes, a nervousness that is quite apparent."

These differences can be seen in gifted adults as well as children. "Gifted Adults: Their Characteristics and Emotions," which appeared in the third volume of *Advanced Development*, is one of the most often cited articles on adult giftedness. In these articles, Annemarie conveys her appreciation of the experience of being gifted from birth to maturity.

Upon reading "Some Thoughts about Piaget and the Young Gifted Child," I was surprised to learn that Annemarie had conducted one of the most important studies of Piaget's theory. She modestly had not called attention to it in our conversations. With co-author, Irving Sigel, one of the leading Piagetian scholars and researchers, Annemarie established that gifted children, at the age of five or even younger, can learn the property of conservation (that is, understand that nothing is lost or gained if the same amount changes in form and appears to look different). This, in itself, is remarkable, since Piaget indicated that children usually cannot conserve until the age of eight, and researchers today still believe that gifted children do not progress through Piaget's stages at a faster rate. But even more important, she developed a method of *teaching* children to conserve, by teaching them the prerequisite skills of multiple classification, seriation, and reversibility. Piagetian scholars maintain that none of these concepts can be taught! Annemarie carefully guided the children to be able to discover these concepts by themselves. Her inductive teaching methods are captured in "Finding the Clue to Children's Thought Processes," which contains actual tapescripts of her interactions with children—a rare and instructive treat in the field. This article appeared in *Young Children* in 1966, and a second article based on the research was published in the *British Journal of Educational Psychology* in the same year, early in the Piagetian movement. While gifted educators remain unaware of the study, it is well-known among child development researchers. In February, 1986, the *Social Sciences Citation Index (SSCI)* declared the second paper a classic, indicating that the article had been cited in over 50 publications, making it the most cited paper ever published in the *British Journal of Educational Psychology*!

There are other fascinating aspects of Annemarie's life that few may know about. For example, Eleanor Roosevelt visited the Roeper City and Country School, was impressed, and invited Annemarie and George to her apartment in Manhattan shortly afterwards. "Sesame Street" might not have existed without Annemarie. The creators of "Sesame Street" consulted with her in designing their grant application, and Annemarie's ideas were influential in getting the program funded. When studying medicine in Vienna, Annemarie lived across the street from Sigmund and Anna Freud, and after consulting with both of them, she became the youngest person accepted to study psychoanalysis with Anna Freud. Unfortunately, the course had to be canceled as both Annemarie and the Freuds were forced to flee Vienna when the Nazis invaded Austria. Her parents, Max and Gertrud Bondy, were well-known progressive educators in Germany, and the private boarding school they founded in Marieneu is still in existence and continuing their creative educational philosophy. Annemarie grew up in that boarding school, and fell in love with her husband-to-be, George, a student in the school, when she was only eleven. They were married 53 years and had three children.

Two years after they emigrated to the United States, Annemarie and George co-founded the Roeper City and Country School in 1941, in Bloomfield Hills, Michigan; it was one of the first private schools in the nation to integrate children of color. They established *The Roeper Review* with the unique purpose (very Annemarie-like) of focusing on the philosophical, psychological, moral, and academic issues relating to the lives and experiences of the gifted and talented—a very different agenda from the other, more empirically oriented journals in the field. Annemarie established the Global Awareness Division of the National Association for Gifted Children and a similar committee for the World Council for Gifted and Talented Children in order "to help educators and students to explore and better understand the complexities, problems and beauty of our planet and to become responsibly involved" (Roeper, 1988, p. 1). Her book, *Educating Children for Life: The Modern Learning Community* (1990), describes the participatory democracy that she created at the Roeper School. Her nonhierarchical administrative model can be found in the article, "Participatory vs. Hierarchical Models for Administration: The Roeper School Experience."

Hers has not been an easy life. A survivor of the Nazi holocaust, Annemarie, along with her parents, was able to escape certain death through the courage of George Roeper, her lifelong friend and husband. They left everything behind and came to America. They brought with them the conviction that they had the personal responsibility to help make this a more peaceful, cooperative planet. Their loss of a homeland was mirrored in a second tragedy. In the fire that swept through Oakland on October 20, 1991, Annemarie was able to save the life of the man who had saved hers, but they lost everything except the clothes on their backs, and George never quite recovered from the shock; he passed away within the year. Loss must deepen the human spirit, for Annemarie has emerged from her losses with renewed determination to fulfill her life's mission. She has a passion to help bring about a fundamental change in human behavior based on recognition of the reality of universal interdependence and the complexities of the human soul.

It is my hope that you will be touched by this book, that it will further your soul's growth, and that you will be inspired to pick up the torch and carry on the important work of Annemarie Roeper. Her mission cannot be accomplished by one person. It will take the dedication of many morally sensitive individuals to come: individuals who recognize the importance of the gifted in the transformation to a humane society and use Annemarie's vision as a catalyst for their life's work. Sincere thanks to Judy Galbraith for appreciating Annemarie and for bringing her work to you.

Linda Kreger Silverman, Ph.D.
Director, Gifted Development Center
Denver, Colorado

References

Columbus Group. Unpublished transcript of the meeting of the Columbus Group, Columbus, OH (July, 1991).

Hollingworth, L.S. "What We Know about the Early Selection and Training of Leaders." *Teachers College Record*, 40, pp. 575–592 (1939).

Piechowski, M.M. "Emotional Development and Emotional Giftedness." In N. Colangelo & G. Davis (Eds.), *Handbook of Gifted Education*. Boston: Allyn & Bacon, 1991, pp. 285–306.

Roeper, A. "Introductory Letter." *Global Visions International Newsletter*, p. 1 (Winter, 1988).

— *Educating Children for Life: The Modern Learning Community*. Monroe, NY: Trillium, 1990.

— Hooper, F.H, & Sigel, I.E., "A Training Procedure for Acquisition of Piaget's Conservation of Quantity: A Pilot Study and Its Replication." *British Journal of Educational Psychology*, 36 (3), pp. 301–311 (1966).

Introduction:
A View from the Inside Out

Writing has been essential to my way of life. It has been my method for organizing my thoughts and expressing my feelings ever since early childhood. Over the last forty years, I have used this medium as a means of articulating the philosophy that my husband, George Roeper, and I developed. This philosophy was manifested in the goals and educational principles of the Roeper City and Country School in Bloomfield Hills, Michigan.

The fire that swept through Oakland, California, on October 20, 1991, destroyed most of the tangible evidence of our past life and work and very nearly took our lives as well. With the death of my husband ten months later, the loss became almost all-encompassing. Included in my loss was everything I had ever written. Much of this material will never be replaced, but thanks to many thoughtful friends and colleagues, the majority of my published writings and speeches have been recovered. They have now become my most precious possessions. They are my link to the past and, with this publication, my link to the future.

The articles, essays, and addresses included in this book represent different aspects of my love for and devotion to the soul of the human being, and my belief in the tenderness with which the soul needs to be nurtured in the context of sensitive global awareness. They embody the vision, the philosophy, and the mission of our lives, as well as theoretical and practical applications. They express my consistently held view of education as the vehicle for self-actualization within the reality of global interdependence. This central theme is illuminated from different angles and elaborated on in relation to the development of personal, national, and global environments.

I have selected those articles, essays, and addresses that were key-stones for my evolving philosophy. They were the seeds for the Self-Actualization, Interdependence model (SAI) that I have described in *Educating Children for Life: The Modern Learning Community* (Trillium

Press, 1990). They encompass education, psychology, and my philosophy of global awareness, all of which are closely interconnected. They mark my personal journey as an educator of young children, an educator of gifted children, a school administrator, and, finally, a global citizen. Throughout my career, I have perceived the necessity of new institutional structures and administrative approaches to fulfill the inner needs of children as well as to reflect the reality of the world. Hierarchical structures are antithetical to the circular organization of nature. Each year of my life, I experience with greater urgency the need to contribute to humanity's realization that we are all interconnected and interdependent with every facet of the world around us.

It is my hope that you will read these articles with the tenderness with which they were conceived, and that they may offer you an expanded perspective of the way you look at children and the world.

Annemarie Roeper
Oakland, California

Editors' Note

ANNEMARIE ROEPER: SELECTED WRITINGS AND SPEECHES brings together a broad and representative array of articles, essays, and addresses spanning Dr. Roeper's life and work. All of the selections included in this volume appear in newly edited form. The close inter-connection of the themes results in some repetition of material from essay to essay. The inevitable redundancies have been kept to a minimum by the selection process: Only those writings and speeches that make a unique point about the subject they treat have been included here. For references to those of Dr. Roeper's writings that do not appear in the present volume, please consult the *Suggestions for Further Reading* at the back of the book. These are not intended to be an exhaustive bibliography of source material on the education of gifted children, but rather reflect the formative influences upon Dr. Roeper's own evolving thought on this subject.

RCM
LKS
PLE

Truth and the Young Child

Unpublished (1972).

> *The result...is almost a conspiracy of silence which is reciprocated by children. It is as though a mutual agreement exists that certain things, even though obvious to all, simply have not occurred. This means that we may believe we have succeeded in keeping certain realities from children, while, in actuality, they have successfully kept their concerns from us. The consequence is that they are forced to deal with difficult problems by themselves and are left to face questions without help, for which they are neither emotionally nor intellectually equipped.*

America is continuously torn apart by riots, disagreement, and disenchantment. Murder, crime, violence, and accidents can be seen on television and heard discussed whenever one cares to listen. If we look back into the past, we find that this state of affairs is not new at all. There have always been wars; there have always been disagreements.

What is the place of the child in such a world? As adults, we wish we could escape from life's problems and not have to face the world as it is. Because we love our children, we have the desire to protect them from the negative aspects of life as long as possible to permit them to have a happy, untroubled childhood. Of course, there are those who feel that children must go through the hard school of life and learn to fight their own battles and solve their own problems without help or support; this is the way they will learn how to cope with life. The philosophy of schools is usually built on the former premise. Most stories written for young children avoid creating anxiety by excluding real conflicts or confrontations. They usually have mild plots and always have happy endings. Fairy tales are frowned upon, and if they are told at all, only modified versions are used that change the original plots, leaving out the scary details and insuring happy endings. Nursery school teachers, as well as parents, have a tendency to protect children from knowledge of any unpleasantness, danger, or cruelty. In fact, the following scene is not unusual at all.

A teacher and her assistant are quietly talking to each other in one corner of the room. "Did you know," says one to the other, "that Martha isn't here this morning because her husband died of a heart attack last night?" The other teacher's expression changes to one of shock and she is about to respond when one of the children, four years old, comes over and says, "Why isn't Mrs. Miller here today?" Both teachers put on a smile and say hesitantly, "Well, she isn't feeling very well today." The child looks at them puzzled, not quite knowing what to think.

On the other hand, there are parents who believe strongly in telling the child everything. I have seen mothers prepare children for a forthcoming operation by describing all the gory details without leaving out one ounce of the blood, pain, sick stomach, loneliness, etc., that the child would be likely to experience. And one could see the child's fear mounting minute by minute.

Which of these two is the best approach to use? Before making any decision about how to handle the truth with a young child, we must determine our goals very clearly. The aim of every good teacher and parent is to give the child the skills and emotional stability to cope with the problems of life. How do we reach this goal? Is keeping the truth away from the child or the "sink or swim" policy better able to develop good coping abilities in the child? My answer is that neither of these methods is designed to give children the necessary skills. The first method does not require that children learn because confrontation with reality is completely avoided. The second also does not help them because they are confronted with a frightening world without being given any tools to deal with it. This is like being told to drive a car without being taught how. Young children neither learn how to swim by being kept away from the water nor by being thrown into it. How do we teach children to swim in the sea of life? They learn by careful, supervised exposure to water and swimming lessons that will give them the skills to keep from drowning.

I would like to share another observation. I believe that the majority of adults, particularly teachers of young children, try to protect children from the unpleasant realities of life, but are we really able to do this? Even if we try hard, can we keep children from knowing the true facts? Let me go back to the example of the two teachers talking about their colleague whose husband had died. The boy who asked, "Why isn't Mrs. Miller here today?," and was told she wasn't feeling well must have reacted to the slightly artificial way in which the answer was given. The child did not know what had actually happened, but he felt that he had been deceived. There is ample evidence that young children are aware of and do react to life as it is, not only to their own personal lives but also to the concerns within their immediate families, such as if Dad lost his job, and even further to national and international events. This is especially true with the graphic depictions of suffering in the television news reports. Even though this is probably evident to most adults, the tendency persists to protect young children from all unpleasantness. Recently, a mother told me that a psychiatrist, with whom she happened to chat socially, expressed alarm over the fact that her seven-year-old son was concerned with the war in Vietnam. He felt that young children should be happy and busy playing, leaving these questions to the adults.

People commonly feel that it is difficult enough for adults to deal with life as it is; how can one possibly expect young children to react constructively to difficult world, family, or personal events? The result of this feeling among adults is almost a conspiracy of silence which is reciprocated by children. It is as though a mutual agreement exists that certain things, even though obvious to all, simply have not occurred. This means that we may believe we have succeeded in keeping certain realities from children, while, in actuality, they have successfully kept their concerns from us. The consequence is that they are forced to deal with difficult problems by themselves and are left to face questions without help, for which they are neither emotionally nor intellectually equipped. Children have a great desire to find solutions to their questions and, therefore, will frequently draw their own conclusions, which may turn out to be incorrect and, at times, even more frightening than the reality.

Since we are aware of the fact that children sometimes know about things even though they were not meant to know them, many teachers have adopted a policy of discussing matters only when young children ask about them. This makes it possible to give them help with issues they raise and to avoid confronting them with concerns that they do not already have. However, this does not always work out as well as we would wish, because many children have become conditioned to be silent on certain matters that are not supposed to be their concern; therefore, they will not feel free to open up to adults about subjects that are often particularly close to their hearts. This method, even though aimed at helping young children, still leaves them alone to deal with just those issues where they need the most help.

Why do children need this support? For two reasons: Intellectually, they cannot handle the complexities of life because they are involved in a developmental growth and learning process in this respect, just as in every other area. As a rule, young children still function on a level that does not provide them with skills necessary to deal with these complexities. Unfortunately, life cannot be presented to them in a tidy, neat, sequential manner. It is impossible to expose young children step-by-step to increasingly more difficult life problems as their ability to deal with them increases. There is no sequential curriculum of life, and the possibility exists that children must face difficult problems prior to their ability to deal with them intellectually and emotionally. Let us take the case of the teacher whose husband died. Coping with the concept of death, with their own and their family's mortality, is one of the unavoidable emotional tasks of childhood. The children will deal with the teacher's husband's death within the context of their intellectual and emotional relationship to mortality.

This, then, is the problem. The goal of parents and educators is to develop methods that equip children intellectually and emotionally to deal with life successfully. The methods generally used are either to withhold the truth as much as possible, or to expose children to difficult problems and let them deal with them as best they can. Since, as a rule, events cannot be successfully kept from young children, the latter method might happen more often than we think, even though we may believe the former. Neither method helps children learn to cope. What approach, then, can be used?

In his book, *The Process of Education*, Jerome Bruner (1960) points out that one can teach children anything at any age as long as it is presented to them in a manner that they can understand. In other words, the adults must learn to communicate with young children, and this they can only do if they have a true understanding of the particular developmental phase in which the child is functioning at the moment. How can we find this out? First, in general, there is much material available on the intellectual development of young children (e.g., Piaget & Inhelder, 1964; Wolff, 1960). Jean Piaget's work is particularly important. Anna Freud (1981) and others have written widely on the emotional development of the young child.

Teachers, I believe, have ample opportunity to learn about the stages young children pass through in their emotional as well as intellectual development, which, in reality, cannot be separated. How can they do this? Actually, by not withholding the truth and by making a point of being honest with children at all times. I know this is easier said than done. This, of course, must always be coupled with giving children the opportunity to react to a given truth by allowing them to talk about it and giving them time for discussion and exchange of ideas. Children must feel that they are free to express their thoughts and feelings without criticism or ridicule. They must feel that they are being taken seriously, that it is all right to show feelings and to make mistakes, and that others feel the same way they do; therefore, they do not have to face these realities by themselves. They must also feel that adults are there to help them and to protect them and to make it possible for them to master the truth emotionally and intellectually. By allowing children free expression of their thoughts and feelings, we adults will have the opportunity to discern their levels of thinking and feeling. This in turn will make it easier for us to help them learn the concepts that are connected with a particular problem and to do and say the things that will make them feel emotionally comfortable on their own level with this particular problem.

Let's go back to the example of the teacher whose husband had died of a heart attack. How could the problem have been approached differently? First of all, it would be essential for these teachers to have an idea of the emotional and intellectual development of the young four-year-old child in dealing with this question. Emotionally, four-year-old children are still very egocentric, and they usually react to events only in terms of their own needs and anxieties. Intellectually, they may be in a period where they are not yet sure what the concept of "husband" means. They know what a father is, but do not understand the role of a husband. They may not even be aware of the fact that the teacher has an existence outside of her role at school. They may not yet be able to understand that one person can function in several different capacities, because that requires the developmental skill of categorizing in multiple ways. Based on this knowledge of child development, the teachers together could develop a plan of action for how to deal with this problem with the children. At the moment when the young child approached them asking about the other teacher, they probably would not yet be prepared to give him a thoughtful and adequate answer. This could be conveyed instead of saying that she wasn't feeling well, which was not true. They might say that something had gone wrong at the teacher's house so that she couldn't come to school, and that later on they would be told more about it. Then the children could be called together in small or large groups and told, in simple and truthful words, what had happened. After this, the children would be given the opportunity to ask questions. From their questions, the teachers would be able to discern the understandings the children had reached as well as their feelings about the situation, and be able to use this information as a basis for responding to the children's awareness.

For example, one of the children might show greater concern about his fear of his own father dying or leaving than with the fact that the teacher's husband had died. After his fears had been addressed, he probably would need an explanation of the role of husbands in general, and then some way of identifying intellectually the concept of a teacher's husband. One of the teachers might illustrate this by means of analogy with her own family. She might explain that if her husband were to die, then her children, like Mrs. Miller's, would be without their Daddy. And now Mrs. Miller's children will need to learn to live without a Daddy. This certainly would elicit emotional reactions because the children would then identify personally with the situation. It might be explained that Mrs. Miller's husband was much older than their fathers, and how rarely something like this happens to young fathers like their Daddies, or whatever the realities of the case might be. But it is important to respond to the children's questions in a truthful manner on their developmental level.

If one can give the children as clear an intellectual understanding of the situation as possible, they will be much better able to develop emotional mastery over the events. Only when they feel that they have the ability to master intellectually and emotionally whatever comes their way will the children feel safe in the world rather than overwhelmed by it. Through this free interchange of ideas, the teacher will also have the opportunity to find out about misconceptions the children have developed in their attempt to find their own solutions, and he or she will be able to rectify and change them, or at least try to help the children come to a more realistic understanding of the world.

How can teachers create an atmosphere of freedom that is so strong that children can really feel free to express themselves? How can they do this when the children may have already learned to keep things to themselves? First of all, I believe that teachers must adopt the principle of not lying to young children. This includes little "white lies" that may seem perfectly harmless at the time. There may be things we do not wish to share with children, of course, but that also could be said to them honestly. There may be things that we have to present to them in a certain manner so that they can understand them, or there may be things that we feel we ought to tell them at a later time. All this can be put in words to children, and I think one can develop techniques of honesty, just as there are many means and many ways of not telling the truth. Another principle that I believe would help create an atmosphere of honesty is the idea of communicating with children as much as possible and sharing small events and experiences with them. This also gives them the feeling that we are telling them the truth rather than trying to hide things from them.

Children are curious about everything around them. They like to understand the causes of adults' actions. Often, we make organizational changes and do not think about explaining them to children, although we may discuss these changes with each other in detail. For instance, on hot summer days, we plan a menu which does not require much cooking, because it is hard for the cook to stand over a hot stove on such days. We are not apt to explain this rationale, yet children may be more impressed with this event than with the stories we read to them that day.

Children love to hear stories about their teachers' personal lives. They often have no concept that teachers exist anywhere but in school. We have all had experiences with the look of bewilderment we encounter when we meet one of our students in the grocery store. Children have difficulties conceiving that teachers are also parents, but they are most interested in learning about this. I used to tell my students about my visits to my children in boarding school, and they would have all sorts of questions. "What is a boarding school? Do you stay there all night?"

To share these kinds of experiences with children has another great advantage. The children become aware of the fact that there are many minor events that create feelings of disappointment, anxiety, fear, aggression, and so forth, in adults as well as in children, and they see how adults learn to cope with these feelings. Hearing about methods adults use to deal with challenges frees children to talk about their own minor problems and see what kinds of solutions there can be for them. In some way, practice in coping with minor events prepares children to deal with major ones and creates strategies for reacting to them, just as being exposed to certain kinds of germs creates an immunity to them which would not have happened if one had been living in a sterilized environment. If, for instance, Mother is occasionally absent from home but the child realizes that she always returns, he or she will be able to cope better with longer absences, such as a vacation. Because of this prior experience, the child will not interpret Mother's departure as desertion. Let me cite a few examples of how we have tried to handle the truth and its consequences at the Roeper City and Country Nursery School.

THE FIRST EXAMPLE

A four-year-old black girl resisted all demands by her white teacher. When asked why she was behaving this way, she did not answer. Finally, acting on a hunch, the teacher asked her, "Don't you like me because I am white?" She could have avoided this confrontation with the truth. Now the child started talking and could hardly stop.

"My mother says white people are bad and they're dirty and they pee in their pants...."

To this, the teacher replied, "But you know that all people are really very much alike. Black people cry when they are sad, so do white people; black children like to play, so do white children."

"No," replied the child, "all people are *not* alike. Girls do not have a penis, but boys do."

The teacher became aware that this child was dealing with many different confusions and concerns at the same time which influenced her behavior. The girl reacted to general racial friction from the level of her intellectual development. According to Piaget's theory, she was at the stage at which she was just beginning to master the concept of classification, and she reasoned that people and things can be either different or alike, but not both. Since she knew boys and girls are different, she also was convinced that black people and white people are different. She could not grasp that people can be both different and alike at the same time. Therefore, she didn't believe that her teacher was telling her the truth. The teacher would not have discovered the source of the child's confusion and resistance had she not tried to be honest.

The child felt some relief at being able to share her thoughts. The problem was by no means solved, but it gave the teacher a better basis for talking with the child's mother and helping the child to resolve the conflicts as well as learn the complex task of multiple classification.

THE SECOND EXAMPLE

The day after Senator Robert Kennedy was killed, the three-year-old children at our school played as usual. I asked the teacher to bring up the subject with the children as a group. She agreed to do so reluctantly, saying to me, "Why do you want to disturb them? They are playing so happily."

Later, she came to me very excited. "I talked to them just because you told me to, but I could hardly believe what happened. It was as if I had turned on a faucet! Every one of the children had something to say about it. They had all seen it on television, and all of them had heard talk about it. Some had a clear understanding of what had happened, while others didn't. One said, 'My brother has been shot.' It was difficult to explain to him that it was somebody else's brother. Others said, 'The police will get him and put him in jail.' 'A bad man killed him.' 'My mother is sad about it.' 'The man at the gas station said it serves him right.' Then I asked them, 'Do you think it served him right? Was he a bad man? If he was a bad man, then would it be right to shoot him?' One child answered, 'The soldiers shoot bad people in the war.' More thoughts and feelings poured out." The teacher wasn't able to answer all of the children's questions, but she admitted to them when she didn't know the answer.

It is more important for children to learn to ask honest questions than it is for them to always receive answers. The children were relieved because the door was open to communicate with the teacher and each other. We informed their parents of these discussions and they continued them at home. One little boy whose own father had died insisted that his mother write a letter to the little Kennedy children telling them that he was sad for them. Another little girl kept lying down and closing her eyes. When her mother asked her what she was doing, she said, "I'm playing dead." She and her mother spent the whole weekend discussing death. The girl had to keep acting it out until she had developed the concept of death to a point that satisfied her. With her mother's help, she was able to develop a more complex idea of death than that of other children, who frequently believe that death is like falling asleep.

A THIRD EXAMPLE

A little boy was in a car accident in which his mother was injured. The school was informed, but when the child returned to school nothing was said about it to the child. After awhile, we noticed that he seemed like a changed person: quiet, withdrawn, apprehensive. Finally, his teacher talked to him and asked him about the accident. His thoughts came rushing out. His mother had been bleeding, he said. He had been separated from her by a policeman. More and more of the story came out. The teacher then discussed his feelings with him. He felt that somehow the accident was his fault. Children often assume that they or someone else are to be blamed whenever a misfortune occurs. This incident led to a general discussion with the class about the meaning of the word "accident." The children said things like, "Something bad happened." "Somebody did something bad." "Someone got hurt." Finally, someone constructed a clear definition of accident: "Something happened but nobody wanted it to happen." For many children, this was a new concept of the meaning of "accident." For the boy in the car accident, it was a tremendous sense of relief to talk about the issue with his classmates and to realize he wasn't responsible for his mother's injury.

Discussions with children are not always easy to conduct. The teacher must take the initiative, but at the same time follow children's important leads. It is best to begin by asking open-ended questions or by first relating an incident that might bring up children's associations with the topic. If the children are really involved, the teacher might be overwhelmed by too many simultaneous responses. Therefore, it is better to conduct discussions in small groups, to ask children to take turns, and, at the same time, allow spontaneity. The quiet child might have to be singled out to answer a question or relate an incident. The outgoing child may have to be quieted. Discussions with young children may not be easy for the teacher to handle, but they can become the backbone of the educational process once they are mastered; they serve as an important tool for learning.

The real difficulty, I believe, is not how to handle the truth with young children, but how to educate ourselves to express it. There is a new honesty among young adults which demands their elders face life realistically, but for many of us "saving face" is a way of life that certainly has its advantages also. Many adults routinely hide the truth to protect the child or to save their own image in the eyes of the child or because they themselves cannot face it. My own son, at the age of five, made the following statement to me: "I never know what to believe because you always tell me my paintings are beautiful." In my eagerness to make him feel secure and capable, I achieved the opposite effect. I made him feel insecure because he sensed that my praise was not based on realistic judgment but on my wish to create an image. One of the most frequent and, I believe, basically destructive customs is to keep a child in a grade in which he or she cannot achieve at the same level as the other children. Daily that child is exposed to his or her inadequacy without the opportunity of really facing the problem and getting help to solve it. In this way, the child is taught to deal with the problem by denying its existence. The same is true if we tell a child that she is big when, in fact, she is really small, or that he was not adopted when he remembers seeing his parents for the first time when he was two years old.

The most difficult falsehood for a child to cope with is when adults around him or her pretend that they can do no wrong. Parents occasionally believe that their authority will be undermined if they admit a mistake. Children learn from this a different lesson than the one intended. They know soon enough when a parent makes a mistake or does not keep a promise, and at the same time they notice that they are being fooled. They infer that it is bad to make a mistake, that it is better to hide it. In fact, they develop a concept—which is close to their infantile logic anyway—namely that things are not as they are, but what they *seem* to be. They grow up to believe that truth is what one sees on the outside. The truth becomes what we say it is, not what the facts are. A hypocrite, I believe, often is not a person who pretends that something is different from what it is, but one who has been raised to believe an act is only real when others know of its existence. This is a perpetuation of the infantile stage before the conscience has developed. At that level, the child relies on the adults' reactions to determine right from wrong because he or she has not yet developed a conscience. The action that parents did not condemn because they did not see it is therefore made nonexistent. Children who live in an environment that is hypocritical do not receive the proper support with which to face reality, and may actually be retarded in their emotional development, never growing up emotionally. In addition, children have a tendency to feel overpowered by adult competencies in comparison to their own incompetence. Every teacher, I am sure, has experienced the excited and relieved laughter of children when she or he has made a mistake and admitted it, such as spilling something, bumping into a table, forgetting something, or breaking a rule. Children need to see adults acknowledging that they, too, make mistakes.

I would like to end by adding a word of caution. As with every other principle, if carried to the extreme, the idea of telling the truth to young children on occasion may be ill-advised. There may be instances when the truth at that moment is unbearable. A few years ago, we had at our school a little girl whose mother had died shortly before she joined us. The child repeated over and over again that her mother was at home, that she had only gone away to the store, that her mother washed her dress every day, and so forth. We felt that the child needed these fantasies for the time being. We did not actively support her fantasizing, but we also did not deny her stories. Slowly, in cooperation with her housekeeper and her father, we helped her accept the truth as she became more capable of coping with it. Even in this case, however, the necessary goal was to face the truth eventually. In fact, it was understood that both the child and the adults knew the reality of the situation and that the child's need to pretend for awhile was also a part of the truth.

All children face the inner task of finding a comfortable place for themselves in this world; they must develop a sense of inner mastery with which to confront whatever life brings. To help them achieve this intellectual and emotional mastery, the adults in their lives need to build a strong, basic trust relationship with them. This can only develop when we relate to them with understanding, empathy, and honesty.

References

Bruner, J.S. *The Process of Education*. Cambridge, MA: Harvard University Press, 1960.

Freud, A. *The Writings of Anna Freud: Volume 8. Psychoanalytic Psychology of Normal Development*. New York: International Universities Press, 1981.

Piaget, J., & Inhelder, B. *The Early Growth of Logic in the Child*. New York: Harper & Row, 1964.

Wolff, P.H. *The Developmental Psychologies of Jean Piaget and Psychoanalysis*. New York: International Universities Press, 1960.

Normal Phases of Emotional Development and the Gifted Child

Published in *The Roeper Review* (June, 1978).

It is by being aware of and understanding how gifted children proceed through these phases of emotional development that we can help them to grow and mature more successfully.

I cannot possibly do justice to the various theories of child development in a single article. There are many schools of thought about such development, and all use different terminology to explain and describe the various phases of children's emotional development. But my topic here is gifted children, not child psychology. Because I am most comfortable discussing psychoanalytic approaches to child development, in this article I will employ that vocabulary to describe the periods of emotional development of gifted children in particular, and how these differ from those of other children.

The first phase in emotional development is the so-called *oral phase*. In this period of development, the newborn baby relates to the world through his mouth, through sucking and nursing. It is the period in which, according to Erik Erikson, the child moves from distrust to trust. He has moved from the protection of the womb to the strange outside world and is a completely dependent human being. The nature of this dependency will form the basis of his relationship to the world if he can trust his relationship to his mother or other caretaker.

From my experience, I have found that almost from the first day some children seem to be more "of this world" than others. These are the gifted children who are born with a greater awareness of and sensitivity to their surroundings and greater cognitive ability. Every step they take in growing is colored by this extended awareness. The young gifted child may have more reasons to trust and more reasons to distrust simply because his perception is more complex. Therefore, both the hope and the danger of a normal and "good" or abnormal and "poor" oral phase of development are present. The child who is gifted will react to more that is happening around him, but may not yet have the language ability or the consciousness to express his reactions to that which he has experienced. There may be many unanswered questions. He may feel lonely, and feelings and reactions may have developed with which he is not able to deal because they are too complicated for him at this stage. Such factors may color this very first phase. On the other hand, he may also be eager to conquer the world and feel the ability to do so because of his intellectual ability. He may, therefore, move more quickly into the next phase, the so-called *anal phase.*

In this period of development, the child learns many skills and gains personal power and some control. This is the time when the child learns give-and-take between himself and others. It is the phase in which the pleasure principle, which controls the first phase (i.e., the only thing that the child knows is that he wants what he wants when he wants it), meets up with the realities of life. The reality principle interferes with the pleasure principle and with his wish fulfillment. Thus, the child finds that he must learn some control and postponement to achieve his desires. At this point, he controls and postpones, not because he has a conscience or a superego, but because he runs into trouble or disapproval from others with whom his wishes interfere.

Several things happen to the gifted child in this second stage of development. He may find it easier to control some of his wishes because he has a better ability to sublimate or substitute a more acceptable form of behavior for a less acceptable one. For instance, in terms of toilet training, the toddler may have more motivation to transfer the normal pleasure of being wet into playing with water and paint and producing some interesting pictures. At the same time, he may gain the same kind of pleasure that he did when he was not yet trained.

Conversely, a gifted child's wish fulfillment might continue beyond the first phase because he has a greater ability to play tricks on his siblings or manipulate his parents. He may learn, for instance, when he wants a toy from his brother, to give him something in one hand and discreetly withdraw the toy he wants from the other. In this situation the child does not have to understand that his brother also has needs that must be considered. He wants only to get around that which interferes with his own needs.

There are some very gifted adults who have never had to give up their self-centeredness and feeling of omnipotence because their intelligence has made it possible for them to fulfill their wishes. I am certain we have all met this kind of person. Because of their intelligence, which enables them to work around situations, these people never learn to realize that they have to share the world, and as a result never develop empathy for others. There is no push toward superego development in persons of this kind.

On the other hand, many gifted children develop a strong conscience because their specific cognitive ability leads them to be aware of reality, to understand the pain of others, and to draw logical conclusions. This kind of awareness, if you will, may develop before their impulses and emotions are mature enough to deal with their insight. They may still have a lack of inner control. For instance, a young gifted child may throw a block across the room before he can control himself. Yet, at the same time, he may develop a feeling of guilt that is somewhat inappropriate for his age level.

This pulling at both ends, of insight and small self-control, may interfere with reaching out further and growing toward independence. It may make a gifted child withdraw to an earlier stage. For instance, a child well past the toilet training years may be more reluctant to control his bowels and to take responsibility for his own actions. For this reason, we often see an excess of anxiety in gifted children at ages three or four. Their reaction to the unknown may become fearful.

It is at this age when children often enter nursery school, and there are many gifted children who face a difficult adjustment in this first entrance into the world away from home. They sense the complexity and dangers of this world and must be permitted to conquer it carefully. They must be allowed to take their time and have the support of parents and teachers. They must never be fooled by parents and teachers. Insecurity becomes unbearable to the gifted child whose mother sneaks out of school on the first day. That child may never trust his mother again.

On the other hand, a child's special ability may also be the reason for a joyous reaching out to the world. The child who knows his intellectual skills and who considers them a property, which he will never lose and which will help him acquire more skills and master the world, will move into greater independence with great enthusiasm. It is always exciting to watch a child like that grow and learn. This child learns with leaps and bounds because the world has proven safe and he has the ability to experience it in all of its complexity. Such drive is beautiful to watch and expresses itself in purposeful activity. It is a kind of activity that many older children and adults never lose.

This drive, coupled with the specific skills of the gifted child, may lead to an early movement into the next stage, which is the so-called *genital phase.* This stage of development marks the period of family romance. When the child has learned so many skills, feels at home away from home, and gains some control over his mind, his emotions, and his body, he may, in fact, begin some academic learning. He begins to feel that he has caught up with the adults in his environment. He begins to feel that he can compete with his father or mother for the love of the opposite sex. It is another period of unreality when the child does not see who he really is, but feels that he is what he wants to be. The child feels that he is capable of doing anything. This, I believe, is a somewhat dangerous period for the gifted child, for he often overestimates himself. He may have good reason to do so, for his ability to solve problems may be equal or superior to that of his parents. His untouched infantile approach may allow for alternatives that are closed to the parents.

The debilitating perfectionism, which we have all noted as one of the most typical characteristics of gifted children, stems from this developmental period. Many parents are often so impressed and identified with their gifted child at this age that they are in awe of him. The child's advice is listened to and taken very seriously. Often the gifted child actually becomes the head of the household. I have seen this happen many times. This creates an enormous burden and problem for the gifted child, for it is emotionally overwhelming for a child to grow up believing that he is responsible for the family. His capability has moved him out of the proper position and kept him from developing normally. This kind of role reversal often happens in a one-parent family. A lonely mother sometimes shares the responsibility for managing the household as well as her personal worries with her young child. She gives him the feeling that he knows the answers and that she depends on him. Again, this child is deprived of his childhood.

On the other hand, parents who are very authoritarian, who insist on being obeyed even when the child knows that they are wrong and fallible, can be devastating to a gifted child. The child may be afraid to grow further. The child may be afraid to develop his real potential because he feels that the parent fears his rivalry. The child actually fears the parents because of what he perceives as competition between himself and them. Thus, the gifted child decides it is better not to learn, even though the parents seem to act as if they want the child to learn. The child feels that he must never be as good in his learning as the parents. This kind of attitude is often the reason for learning blocks in gifted children.

Phyllis Greenacre, a psychoanalyst who has written about the development of gifted children, believes that the gifted child never gives up the family romance—that he moves directly from the love of the parent to the love of humankind or the love of his own ability. From her writings, I am under the impression that Dr. Greenacre feels that many gifted people are not as capable of loving a person as they are of loving their own ability and their duty to humankind. Again, however, the gifted child may move through this developmental phase into the next period, which is the *latency phase*, more smoothly than the average child.

The gifted child is more likely to realize the process of growth, for he understands that he has the skills to learn and grow and that one day he will be able to live as an adult. This is what he will be working on during the latency phase, a period of less stress. This is another period in which the child understands his own realistic situation. It is a time of learning and growth, a time when the child identifies with his peers, usually those of the same sex. The gifted child often enters this period at an early age and moves out of it early into adolescence. Sometimes, however, I get the feeling that they almost skip the latency phase. Yet it is obvious that the gifted child makes special spurts in early and late latency. Being freed from family involvement, his specific skills may come to the fore at this level, and everything in the world around him becomes exciting and worth knowing.

At this point, the child moves into the developmental period of adolescence. Parents and teachers play a highly significant role in the way a gifted child may go through this phase of emotional development. Adolescence is the interval between childhood and adulthood. It is the period when the child moves back and forth between the two worlds. There are times when it is important for the child to feel that he can depend on his parents. There are also times when a child needs to prove his independence. We used to feel that a child's dependency was based on a belief that parents are omnipotent, able to know and do all. However, at an early age the gifted child realizes that his parents are simply human beings, that they have problems for which they may not know all the answers. This in no way means that the gifted child no longer needs the support of his parents. It simply means that he may question his parents' attitudes, actions, and beliefs. Parents must understand that this is not defiance on the child's part, but rather a sign of maturation and the sorting out of the complexities of life.

In my work with gifted children, I have always been impressed by how well they know their teachers, both in terms of their good qualities and their shortcomings. I have also found that if adults insist on being placed on a pedestal, children will lose their trust and respect for them. They may even try to manipulate and deceive them. If, on the other hand, adults reveal themselves as being fully human, display an honest desire to fulfill children's needs, and are thoughtful of them, then children will respect adults and the knowledge they bring to life through their experience. Moreover, gifted children will trust these adults. This is particularly true for gifted children, who expect trust with adults to be a mutual regard as human beings, one with superior experience, the other with a need for support.

We all have a somewhat similar concept of the phases of development, from the absolutely dependent infant who is completely egocentric to the relatively independent adult who sees himself as a member of society. Most of us agree that much can happen to an individual on this road from infancy to adulthood. Roadblocks of all sorts can be put in the way of the child in the form of fate and inner and outer experiences. A child can remain fixated on any one of these phases and never, or only with help, grow beyond it. A child can develop neurotic symptoms during a phase and may need help to go through it. Or a child can sail through the various phases with a minimum of problems and fully develop his personality. I say "a minimum of problems," for problems are always a part of life, and are necessary for the movement from one developmental phase to another. The gifted child will pass through these phases, as does every other child, but his giftedness will bring changes and deviations to the developmental phases. It is by being aware of and understanding how gifted children proceed through these phases of emotional development that we can help them to grow and mature more successfully.

Reference

Greenacre, P. *Emotional Growth: Psychoanalytic Studies,* Vol. II. New York: International Universities Press, 1971. From the chapter, "The Childhood of the Artist."

Finding the Clue to Children's Thought Processes

Co-authored with Dr. Irving Sigel. Published in *Young Children* (formerly *The Journal of Nursery Education*), Vol. XXI, No. 6 (September, 1966), pp. 335–348. Portions were read at the combined meeting of the National Association for the Education of Young Children (NAEYC) and the Ontario Association for Nursery Education (OANE) in Toronto (May, 1964) by Annemarie Roeper. The research project was reported by Dr. Sigel at the conference, "New Media in Educating Business and Industry," Wayne State University, Detroit, Michigan (January, 1965).

The method used was the inquiry method. The children were never simply informed of a concept but were guided to discover it themselves through observation and discussion. The three processes described by Piaget were each introduced through simple examples. Each process was discussed and pointed out by different methods until the children's comments seemed to reflect a real understanding.... The ability to conserve can be reached through the process of growth but can be facilitated by carefully planned education.

For centuries, people have been both amused and impressed by children's remarks and observations. Nothing is more popular than quotations "out of the mouths of babes." Nursery school educators are familiar with such remarks as "I know there are monsters in outer space, because I saw them on television," or "The whale is going to eat me," or "I see your Daddy," meaning the teacher's husband. But also, "I have a shadow, because light cannot shine through a thing, except for glass," or "Infinity is more than anything else."

Adults may chuckle at these childish expressions of foolishness or wisdom, but children are deeply convinced of their conclusions. This becomes obvious to anybody who has ever tried to change a child's mind about something he deeply believes in. The little boy, who knows there are monsters in outer space, may suffer from real fears. But much as he would like to be relieved of them, he will not accept the adult correction of his concept. Why not? Is it that the adults lack the clue to his reasoning? Is it that we do not know by what route he has arrived at his conclusion and therefore cannot bring any argument that will contradict his thinking? Perhaps we cannot prove anything to a child according to his own logic until we can understand his thought processes. Perhaps in this case we can only offer our protection from the monsters or get him to accept our thinking by virtue of our authority, not by our ability to convince him. Possibly we are not sharing a language of thought, and if this is true, it would constitute a serious lack of communication between adult and child that would pervade every area of contact. Until we find an answer to this fundamental question, our intellectual communication with children will continue to be based on trial-and-error rather than on active mutual understanding. Through advances in psychology, we have learned to identify with the child's feelings. Through learning about his cognitive style, we may understand his "thoughts."

This article is concerned with an exploration of the following questions:

1. Do children actually have a different method of thinking?

2. What is their method?

3. Do all children use the same method?

4. Does children's style of thinking follow a definite sequence of development until it reaches the stage of abstract thinking used by adults?

5. Does each child reach this point only as he matures, or can this process be influenced, that is, accelerated or slowed down, by outside forces?

We believe that the answers to these questions will give us some insight into:

- children's reactions to daily life situations
- unexpected emotional responses in children
- methods of daily communication with the young child
- the child's approach to academic learning
- ways in which to predict learning ability
- ways in which to support learning ability
- timing of teaching
- methods of teaching

- choice of subject matter in teaching
- other aspects of teacher training
- other aspects of parent education.

We will begin with an example showing how different "intellectual conversations" may influence children's reactions to an experience: John's family owns a puppy. John is about four years old. Blacky has been his constant companion and is being referred to as Blacky Jones, just as he himself is known as Johnny Jones. One day the family car, parked on a hill, rolls backward and kills the puppy, who was sitting behind it. John is heartbroken. His mother tries to make him feel better, explaining that it was an accident. Someone forgot to pull the brakes, and so the car, rolling backward, ran over Blacky and killed him. Blacky should not have been sitting behind the car. When Mother sees that John is still very unhappy, she tells him that they may be able soon to get another dog just like Blacky.

How well does John understand what his mother is trying to tell him? How well is he equipped to understand the meaning of this experience?

Does John know what death means? Does he know what life means? How can he arrive at these concepts? Is everything that moves alive? Then the car that killed Blacky must be alive also and must have decided to do it. The car might want to kill him, John, too, if he did something that was against the rules. Does John understand that human beings can only produce human beings? Or does he think Blacky Jones is as much a member of his family as he is? In that case, if he (John) was run over, would his parents soon get a new boy and forget him? How much do *we* know of his real thoughts and concepts?

One can find enormous variation in children's reactions to similar situations:

1. John may be deeply convinced that Blacky is a true member of the family, that the car is alive and therefore may decide to run over him also, and that his parents then might easily replace him. Thus the incident would create not only feelings of grief over his loss, but also strong fear of personal rejection. Since he identifies completely with the dog, he feels great anxiety in addition to this grief.

2. John may have come to no conclusion, one way or another, about the identity of Blacky and of the car. (This is rare, and the fact that it is rare signifies an important matter to be discussed more fully later, namely, that the child as a rule feels compelled to solve problems in some way. He wants to master his surroundings. He may therefore more likely arrive at a wrong conclusion than at no conclusion.)

3. John may believe the true and false at the same time (without being disturbed about it), leaning more toward one concept of mind than the other, depending on his frame of mind. He might feel at one moment that Blacky is his brother, while at the same time he may be aware that this is not true. His feelings also would vacillate.

4. John may have a true understanding of the situation. This would mean that he realizes Blacky was only a pet in the home—one who was loved but was not identified with him as a person in any way. He also knows, then, that the car is not alive, that it ran over the dog by accident, and that there was no purpose behind the incident. In this case, he can view the incident realistically and concentrate his feelings where they actually belong, namely, in grief over the loss of his dog.

Why do we encounter this great variety of reactions? Again, we find ourselves at a loss for an explanation, because we are only able to observe the end results of a thought process, not the road the child travels to arrive at his conclusions. In order to understand what the child thinks or why he thinks the way he does, we must find out *how he thinks and what method he uses.*

Jean Piaget, the Swiss psychologist, has done a great deal of research for many years to find the answers to these questions. Other psychologists have recently become interested in this area of investigation and have checked Piaget's work by repeating his experiments as well as elaborating on them. The results of these investigations are, of course, well known, but they have not generally been applied to our specific inquiry.

Is the infantile method of thinking different from the adult? Does the ability for logical thought develop in a predetermined order? Will the conclusions the child arrives at change according to the different stages he reaches during this process? Piaget answers these questions in the affirmative, and these contentions have been validated by Flavell (1963), Hunt (1962), Elkind (1961), and Lovell (1961), and by many others. There seems no doubt that the child's growth in thinking follows a certain predetermined sequence and that he cannot skip any of the developmental steps involved (Piaget, 1964; Piaget & Inhelder, 1964).

What is the predetermined sequence in which the child's capacity for logical thought grows? According to Piaget, this begins with the so-called *preoperational* stage, within which the child goes through several predetermined steps until he reaches the *operational* stage, which is the ability of the adult to think in the abstract.

One basic prerequisite for abstract thinking is the ability to classify. How does a child attack this task? Here again, he goes through different steps within the preoperational stage. In the beginning, he is unable to use any significant criteria in order to put things into classification. Piaget and Inhelder, in their book, *The Early Growth of Logic in the Child,* use the following example: A young child is asked, "What is a mother?" He may answer, "A mother is a lady who cooks supper." Or, to use our example, "Is a dog your brother?" may be answered by "Yes, because he lives in the same house." In other words, this child is not yet able to solve many of his daily problems intellectually because he does not have the mental tools that are necessary.

The next step shows a little more organization. A child is given a variety of different colored geometrical forms and told to put together those forms that are alike. He may put all red triangles in a row, then when he runs out of red triangles, add red circles, and when he runs out of red circles, add blue ones. He is able to use one single classification— namely, the alikeness of the red triangles. Then, forgetting his original criteria, he adds the red circles, and when there are no more red ones, again changing the criterion, he adds blue circles, which have nothing in common with the original red triangles. Yet this child has kept a significant criterion in mind and has applied it to several objects, namely, the alikeness of form or color, but he will move from one classification to another and forget the original classification.

This child is still not able to understand the story of Blacky. He might still believe that Blacky is his brother because he lives in the same house, if this is his criterion for being a member of the family. If, however, it has been pointed out to him through various examples that people's brothers can only be people, he might find the correct solution by applying this realistic concept to his own situation rather than the incorrect concept he used before. In other words, the criterion has changed. "Put those things that are red together" can be the same as "put those things that are people together," rather than "those that live in the same house." He knows what people are from experience, just as he has learned what red is. This does not mean, of course, that he now understands family relationships or has acquired the skills to figure them out.

Jerome Bruner (1960) and his coworkers, in *The Process of Education,* maintain that children are often able to function in specific areas, such as mathematics, on a level of thinking above that which they are capable of in general. The children could collect certain geometrical forms on the basis of color, but could not translate this classification to other life situations unless the criterion was specifically pointed out. They were taught one criterion and understand the concept in the particular context. This is an example of *single classification.*

The next step is the understanding of *multiple classification* and its application. The child at this stage has learned to put things together according to two or more criteria. He realizes that a geometrical figure can be both red and square. He can now put all the red squares with each other, or with forms that are square, or forms that are red, and can separate them using the same criteria.

John can now classify Blacky with his family when referring to all living beings in his home, but not when human beings are the criterion. For this reason, Blacky could not be John's brother. John has learned the concept of multiple classification and he can apply this to some life situations, but others he will still be unable to classify. Further mental operations are necessary.

One of these operations is understanding the concept of *reversibility*. This is the phenomenon of characteristic things returning to their original condition: $5 + 3 = 8$; $8 - 3 = 5$. An original situation can be re-created as long as no basic aspect has been changed. A child may turn a table upside down and use it as a boat, but since no change has been brought about in "tableness," it remains a table and can be used as one again by turning it right side up, back to its original condition. A black-and-white reversible skirt is still both black and white even though only the white may be visible at the moment. By reversing it, the black will be seen unchanged. To apply the concept to our example, Blacky was born a dog and this condition does not change, even though he lives with a family of human beings.

Another mental operation is the concept of *seriation*. Seriation means that things can be ordered. The child understands that things can be graduated from larger to smaller or vice-versa. Seriation of objects can be based not only on their size but on any other common property that can be graduated along a continuum. For example, colors can be graduated on the basis of saturation or brightness.

When the child has mastered all these different operations, he has reached the stage at which he can understand the concept of *conservation*. Conservation, a term used by Piaget, can be thought of as the ability to think in abstract terms. It marks the beginning of the operational stage. Conservation can be defined as "the cognition that certain properties (quality, number, length, etc.) remain invariant (are conserved in the face of certain transformations) displacing objects or object parts in space, sectioning an object into pieces, changing shapes, etc." (Flavell, 1963, page 245). For example, quantity does not change, even though the form in which it appears does change: A piece of paper crumpled up contains the same amount of paper as before it was crumpled. Nothing has been added or taken away.

Piaget uses the following experiment to ascertain whether children are able to conserve quantity. The examiner takes two round balls of clay that are of equal size, weight, and volume. He then changes the one in front of the child's eyes into a cup-shaped object which looks bigger than the original ball. If the child understands conservation, he will be able to see that nothing has been added or taken away—the original volume, amount, or weight cannot have changed. In order for the child to understand this concept, he must understand that objects can have more than one classification—in fact, he must have the concepts of multiple classification, reversibility, and seriation.

In other words, the child must understand, first, that a piece of clay may acquire different shapes without changing its original qualities. Second, he must understand that it can be changed into one form and back again to the original form. Third, he must understand that, even if it looks bigger as compared to its previous shape, nothing has been added or taken away. In other words, the child must draw his conclusions according to a concept of reality, according to certain orderly laws that he has become aware of, and he must not let visual evidence overrule his judgment. John can now understand that Blacky was like a member of the family in some respects but not in others. Nothing of his dogness has changed. He conserves his dogness, although other qualities are evident. Even though the car moved downhill, nothing of the fact that it is an object, and not a living being, has changed, because these things are governed by natural laws that one knows and are not only determined by what one sees. He realizes, therefore, that the car could not decide to run over him. Since Blacky is not his brother, he can be sure that his parents would not react to his loss in the same way as they did to the loss of Blacky. He would understand that replacing Blacky would imply nothing about himself. This knowledge would keep him from identifying with Blacky too much.

If John had developed the incorrect concept described earlier, he would have an additional task to perform before being able to look at the circumstances with complete realism and before learning to build his concept on the important criteria. Not only must he believe what he knows rather than what he sees, he must also accept the fact that his previous way of thinking was wrong. It is in the absence of this last step that we occasionally find a child who cannot reconcile contradiction for a while, until he becomes completely convinced of the true facts of a situation.

Piaget also notes that conservation occurs at different times in different areas. Children can first understand the conservation of a substance, then weight, and then volume. This sequence of development has generally been verified with some qualifications in studies by Elkind (1961), Kooistra (1963), Lovell (1961), and Smedslund (1961).

The next question follows: Granted that these stages appear according to a certain order of development, are the ages at which they appear also definite, or is there variation in this respect?

With regard to this question, the results of different researchers differ greatly. According to Piaget (1964), conservation appears between the ages of eight and twelve, while Smedslund (1961) and Kooistra (1963) have reported it at younger ages. Kooistra, working with gifted children at the Roeper City and Country School, where children had IQs of 130 or higher, finds it as early as the age of four in a small number of children. This fact in itself is important for the program planning of nursery school teachers and teachers of early elementary school, because these children perhaps can understand material that might previously have been considered beyond their scope.

The question that follows is: Can children be trained in these thinking tasks, or is it merely a matter of maturation which cannot be influenced by education? Studies investigating the induction of conservation of other properties such as number (Beilen & Franklin, 1962; Wohlwill & Lowe, 1960) have shown that training in conservation is generally a failure (Flavell, 1963).

From these studies, the general consensus, then, is that the training of children to conserve, be it quantity or number or area, is very difficult and for the most part results in failure. Flavell contends that these failures indicate that the training for conservation is built on a hollow core and, further, that these failures give evidence for the proposition that Piaget's concepts are not amenable to laboratory training (Flavell, 1963). In looking more deeply into these results, we found that these investigators tried to teach conservation itself. Their failure might be explained by the method of approach rather than by a true inability of young children to acquire these concepts through training. Teaching conservation itself might fail because this would mean skipping some of the necessary prerequisite steps. The purpose of our investigation was therefore to determine whether the ability to conserve could be produced by training the child in the prerequisites: multiple classification, reversibility, and seriation.

We worked with two groups of ten gifted children each ranging in age from 4.9 to 5.1 (see tables I and II on page 34). In each study five of these children were in the training group and five were in the control group. During the course of the first study three children dropped out for unrelated reasons. The mean IQ, as measured on the Stanford-Binet, was 149 for the training group and 152 for the control group. All the children were enrolled as regular students in our nursery school for gifted children, which had an enriched curriculum. These children had been studying a number of concepts. Some of them could read, and the atmosphere could generally be classified as intellectually stimulating.

Teaching Procedure

The experiment group met with Mrs. Roeper three times a week for three weeks for about 20 minutes each session. The method used was the inquiry method. The children were never simply informed of a concept but were guided to discover it themselves through observation and discussion. The three processes described by Piaget were each introduced through simple examples. Each process was discussed and pointed out by different methods until the children's comments seemed to reflect a real understanding. It was impressive to observe the moment of recognition in one child, who was then able to convince the next. Where the children seemed to have grasped the idea in a specific context, other similar situations were introduced, and finally they were led into generalizing their newly found understanding. Verbalizing, according to Jerome Bruner (1960), can protect the child against being overwhelmed by superficial and erroneous visual evidence. In other words, the discussion itself helps the child toward acquiring the ability to conserve.

We will describe each concept covered by examples taken from the verbatim transcript of our discussion.

A Verbatim Session on Classification

Teacher: Can you tell me what this is, Mary?
Mary: A banana.
Teacher: What else can you tell me about it?
Mary: It's straight.
Teacher: It's straight. What else?
Mary: It has a peel.
Teacher: It has a peel.... Tom, what can you tell me about it?
Tom: Ummm.... It has some dark lines on it.
Teacher: Uh-huh.
Tom: It has some green on it.
Teacher: What can you do with it?
Tom: You can eat it!
Teacher: That's right! ... Now let's...
Children: I love bananas!
Teacher: What is this?
Children: An orange.
Teacher: Is it really an orange?
Children: Uh-huh...yes.
Teacher: Look at it closely.
Child: It's an artificial one.
Teacher: Oh, that's right, it's an artificial one.... But what else can you tell me about it?

Children:	You can eat it...it's round.
Teacher:	Uh-huh.
Children:	Orange.
Teacher:	That's right!
Child:	It has a stem.
Teacher:	Now, look at this one. What is this?
Children:	An orange...orange.
Teacher:	And what can you do with it?
Children:	You can eat it...and it's round.
Teacher:	It's round....
Child:	It has a peel....
Teacher:	It has a peel.... Now look at these two things. Are they the same?
Children:	No!
Teacher:	What's different?
Children:	This one...this one here is pressed in on the side a little...this one is lighter.
Teacher:	Do you know what this really is? This is a tangerine...and this is an orange. Now tell me, in what ways are they alike?
Children:	This one is smaller and that's bigger.
Teacher:	I said, in what ways are they alike?
Children:	They are both round...they both have a stem...both orange.
Teacher:	They both have a stem. Both round, both orange. Anything else alike about them?
Child:	They're both fat.
Teacher:	Uh-huh. What can we do with them?
Children:	We can eat them.
Teacher:	We can eat them. Now tell me, what's the same about all of these things?
Child:	These are round, but this isn't.
Teacher:	I said, what is the same about them, not what's different about them.
Children:	They're both round...they're round...they're round...and they are both artificial.
Teacher:	They are all artificial and...are they round?
Child:	No.
Teacher:	What about the banana?
Child:	It's straight.
Teacher:	But...tell me something else that is the same about all of those things.
Child:	They have...all have a peel.
Teacher:	That's right, too. But what can you do with all of them?
Children:	You can eat them!

Teacher:	That's right! That's the same about every one of them. Do you have a name for all of them?
Children:	Yes!
Teacher:	What?
Child:	A banana.
Teacher:	A banana? No...is there something that you can call *all* of them?
Children:	Fruit...fruit.
Teacher:	And what's the same about all fruit?
Children:	They are all round except bananas.
Teacher:	No...why do you call all of these things fruit?
Children:	Because you can eat them.
Teacher:	You can eat them.
Children:	And they are food.
Teacher:	And they are food.

As you can see, we began by labeling the objects presented—bananas, oranges, or whatever—and we continued by discussing the differences, since differences can be grasped by young children before similarities. They moved from insignificant observations to significant ones. We then continued with discussion of similarities until the significant similarity was reached that made it possible to put them all in one important classification.

Another session was used to learn multiple classification. The discussion led to these conclusions: A pencil can be red and can be used for writing. When you need red objects, you put the pencil into the pile for red things; when you need to write, you put it into the pile for writing utensils. Yet it is still only one pencil. Different classification does not change this at all. The multiple classification was acted out and tried out in many different ways. For example, different objects were put in the middle of the table. Each child was told to collect certain objects that belonged together. One child was to take everything red—another, everything that writes. They found themselves reaching for the same object, which proved the point. From there we moved to the generalization: An object can be two things at the same time. This means: A person can be two things at the same time. Therefore, you can be a son and a brother at the same time.

The same method was used to show reversibility. Each child received five pennies. There were five children. They counted all their pennies and then were asked to put them in the middle of the table. The first comment was, "It is more"; then, doubtfully, "It looks like more." Now they were asked, if each child were to take five pennies back, would there be any left on the table? The reaction was doubt and confusion.

Next, the experiment was repeated with five pennies only. This time the process was obvious. They could see it better. Once they were convinced of the situation, the same procedure was used with the larger number of pennies. Objects can be grouped in different ways but can always return to their original form if nothing has been added or taken away. Thus the children were able to realize that sometimes things seem different from what they are.

Seriation

Seriation was approached again in a similar manner. By this time, the children were already aware of the method, and were able to react in a faster and more sophisticated fashion. Can a block be big and little at the same time? The first answer was still no. It was pointed out that visually this is possible. This was then generalized, and then again specified, by showing that a person can be big and little at the same time—big compared to a small child, small compared to a big man.

It became apparent to us that it is important to prove these concepts by many different examples, and to carry out with the children the thought processes that lead from the particular to the general and back again. Verbalizing and clarifying these processes made the children familiar with them and enabled them to apply the same processes independently. It seemed that being able to generalize did not automatically mean that the child could generalize to a new particular situation, but once he has experienced the process, he is better able to do it for himself.

Although the samples were small, the change in the training groups was most interesting and seemed significant. The degree to which the training experiences were assimilated by the training group is reflected in the type of response given to the inquiry questions in the post-training session. The children verbalized their explanations in an articulate way, employing statements of reversibility, for example, as explanations. The explanations were of the level expected as a consequence of the training experience. On the other hand, with the children who did not have any training, there was little change in the explanatory level in the post-training test situations.

All the children were given the conservation tasks of continuous quantity (Plasticene) substance, weight, and volume, and also the continuous liquid task. The procedure was the standard procedure described by Piaget and Inhelder (1964). The results are shown in the tables that follow.

TABLE I

Successes and Failures of Training and Control Groups on Conservation of Quantity Tasks

A. Training Group

	Pre-training				Post-training			
Subjects	Substance	Liquid substance	Weight	Volume	Substance	Liquid substance	Weight	Volume
Gail	0	0	0	0	+	0	+	+
Tom	0	0	0	0	0	+	0	0
Martha	+	0	0	0	+	0	+	0
Mary	0	0	0	0	+	0	0	0

B. Control Group

	First Testing				Second Testing			
Ma	0	0	0	0	0	0	0	0
Je	0	0	0	0	0	0	0	0
Em	+	+	0	0	+	+	+	+

TABLE II

Successes and Failures of Replication Training and Control Groups on Conservation of Quantity Tasks

A. Training Group

	Pre-training				Post-training			
Subjects	Substance	Liquid substance	Weight	Volume	Substance	Liquid substance	Weight	Volume
Ruth	0	0	0	0	+	+	+	0
Joby	0	0	0	0	0	0	0	0
Nelson	0	0	0	0	+	0	0	0
Jody	0	0	0	0	+	+	+	0
Tracy	0	0	0	0	0	0	+	0

B. Control Group

	First Testing				Second Testing			
Al	0	0	0	0	0	0	0	0
Su	0	0	0	0	0	0	0	0
Car	0	0	0	0	0	0	0	0
Ja	0	0	0	0	0	0	0	0
Ji	0	0	0	0	0	0	0	0

Further research is, of course, necessary, but it is our contention that the training procedure may be one method that can help children toward the achievement of conservation, which means toward the abilities of realistic and abstract thinking.

These results and those of Piaget and of other researchers point to the following conclusions:

1. The development of logic in all young children proceeds according to definite stages.

2. The ability to conserve, that is, rational and abstract thinking, may appear as early as the age of four in gifted children who have not been exposed to any systematic training. In most children, however, this so-called operational stage appears through experience at a later age.

3. Even in the preoperational stage, some kind of primitive sequential thought processes appear that may lead the child to either wrong or correct conclusions, depending on what criterion he happens to use. In the early part of the preoperational stage, he may not be capable of understanding a significant criterion, because here again he will make use only of the most obvious. A little later on, however, his experience may make it possible for him to apply another obvious but more important criterion in order to come to more realistic appraisals of situations. It is important to realize that at no stage is his mind inactive. For psychological reasons, he attempts mastery at any level, and if his tools are primitive ones, his conclusions may also be primitive.

4. Training in prerequisites built on whatever stage at which the child actually functions also facilitates growth toward the ability to conserve.

5. The child may be taught to comprehend some of these concepts in specific instances, even though he may not have reached this particular stage in his general development.

In summary, we can make three important points:

A. Children's thought processes differ basically from those of the adult.

B. Children's ability to think logically and abstractly, to conserve, develops according to definite stages.

C. The ability to conserve can be reached through the processes of growth but can be facilitated by carefully planned education.

What do these phenomena mean in terms of early childhood education? Their greatest importance lies in the fact that they open the door to mental territory so far largely unknown and uncomprehended: the young child's intellectual mind. The new discoveries possible seem unlimited. This knowledge can throw new light on specific situations, as well as add new dimensions to our general educational plans.

Knowledge of the type of cognitive style used by young children will help us understand certain puzzling behavior patterns and emotional reactions. The problem of sibling rivalry, for instance—one of the most difficult and universal problems of early childhood—gains another dimension of understanding if seen in this context. A young child may not only feel emotionally rejected when his mother pays attention to a sibling, but he may also be "intellectually" convinced that she cannot possibly love both of them at the same time, since he can only conceive of single classification. He believes that she cannot possibly be both his and his brother's mother simultaneously. If we understand this reaction, we may be able to find ways to help him at least toward a better intellectual grasp of the situation, and this may then to some extent relieve his emotional reaction.

Another case in point: A young child may be completely surprised at the adult's negative reaction when he takes something off a shelf in the dime store. He may not have reached the point at which he can put things into different categories. He therefore has no concept of ownership or "stealing," and cannot possibly understand why his mother thinks a policeman would be angry at him.

These examples may show us why it can be difficult for children to deal successfully with many life situations before some important concepts have been clarified. Knowledge of children's cognitive style may therefore lead to conscious intellectual guidance by the adult that provides the child with the correct clue to help him understand a specific situation even before he has reached the age of conservation.

The following experiment with a group of four-year-olds may prove this point. Most of the children seemed to function on different levels with the preoperational stage. As explained in the Blacky story, the concept of what is alive is a most basic one in the child's daily life experiences. We therefore tried to give the children conscious guidance in understanding this concept. These children were in the habit of discussing problems with their teacher. Through the discussion method, she was able to find out what their own concepts were, and then guide them into their own discovery of usable criteria for more realistic conceptualization. The discussion method was amplified by movies, visits to a farm, books, and so on. We can only give here an overview of the procedure without describing the approach in great detail.

In order to find out the children's thinking in regard to the subject of "aliveness," the teacher would ask such questions as, "Is a book alive?" One of the answers to this inquiry was, "No, it cannot move." In this case, single classification (things that are alive move) leads to the correct answer. But it is precisely this concept built on single classification that brought an incorrect answer to the next question: "Is a car alive?" "Yes, because it moves." In this case, a second classification is required and was finally arrived at by another child: "A car is not alive. It moves but cannot start itself." Out of this, then, emerged the following definition, which required the child's functioning within the concept of multiple classification: Things can move whether they are alive or not, but only things that are alive can do both—can move and can move by themselves. Other categories were then added: Only things that are alive can grow and reproduce; and so forth. The children were then able to add categories of their own: "A cow is alive—it is made of flesh and blood; a car is not—it is made of steel." Or: "A cow is alive—it makes moo when he feels like it; a car is not alive—it can only sound its horn when you push it."

A second group of the same age and background was exposed to the same experiences—the same movies, stories, visits to the farm, and so on—but not to this specific type of discussion. These children were not able to give accurate definitions of aliveness. The first group was able to develop specific useful concepts based on the specific guided approach.

This brings up the issue of *incidental learning.* The young child is most eager for learning. Every experience, therefore, becomes a learning experience. Early childhood education has realized the child's great potential for learning by himself, and it has become an integral part of preschool education. This type of learning, however, is unselective in the case of the child who functions on a preoperational level. He is not yet equipped to differentiate between different categories of facts and therefore to build his judgment on proper relevancy. In consequence, he is apt to develop misconceptions, such as: A car is alive because it moves. Such conceptions may become deeply embedded in the child's thinking and stand in the way of further concept formation. In other words, the young child is deeply motivated toward understanding the world but is not yet mentally equipped for it. The only solution for this dilemma seems to be knowledgeable adult guidance. It is for this reason that we believe the young child should be helped toward proper concept formation through an organized goal-directed approach built on knowledge of his cognitive style. The method described here may offer one approach.

Understanding children's cognitive style may provide an explanation for the failure of certain children to understand simple mathematical concepts. It may at the same time provide the means to help them overcome their problem. In addition, it may provide a method of keeping such failures from occurring.

The greatest obstacle to such an approach to education is that it is most difficult for the adult to identify with the young child's manner of thinking. We have forgotten thoughts of early childhood, just as we cannot recall the feelings of that period. It actually requires translation of our method of thinking into another thought language. It may be difficult to learn a foreign language, but the more familiar we become with this one, the better we will understand the children, and, realizing our previous lack of communication with them, the more areas we will find that are affected by this new understanding.

In this article, we were able to touch only briefly on some of the many possible applications of Piaget's concepts in our pilot study. Nevertheless, we hope that it will stimulate other educators toward finding new ways of coordinating research results and education in this far-reaching field.

References

Beilin, H., & Franklin, I.C. "Logical Operations in Area and Length Measurement, Age and Training Effects." *Child Development*, 33, p. 607–616 (1962).

Bruner, J. S. *The Process of Education*. Cambridge, MA: Harvard University Press, 1960.

Elkind, D. "Quantity Conceptions in Junior and Senior High School Students." *Child Development*, 32, pp. 551–560 (1961).

Flavell, J.H. *The Developmental Psychology of Jean Piaget*. Princeton, NJ: Van Nostrand, 1963.

Hunt, J. McV. *Intelligence and Experience*. New York: The Ronald Press, 1962.

Kooistra, W. *Developmental Trends in the Attainment of Conservation, Transitivity, and Relativism in the Thinking of Children: A Replication and Extension of Piaget's Ontogenetic Formulations*. Unpublished doctoral dissertation, Wayne State University, Detroit, Michigan, 1963.

Lovell, K. *The Growth of Basic Mathematical and Scientific Concepts in Children*. New York: Philosophical Library, 1961.

Piaget, J. *The Child's Conception of Numbers* (3rd ed.). London: Routledge & Kegan Paul, 1964.

—& Inhelder, B. *The Early Growth of Logic in the Child*. New York: Harper & Row, 1964.

Smedslund, J. "The Acquisition of Conservation of Substance and Weight in Children. II. External Reinforcement of Conservation of Weight and of the Operation of Addition and Subtraction." *Scandinavian Journal of Psychology*, 2, pp. 71–84 (1961).

Wohlwill, J.G., & Lowe, R.C. "Experimental Analysis of the Development of the Conservation of Number." *Child Development*, 33, pp. 153–157 (1960).

Some Thoughts about Piaget and the Young Gifted Child

Roeper Publications, Professional Section, November, 1977.

All of the above serves to support the paradox that gifted children are in many ways like other children, but there also exists a basic difference in the quality of their thinking and feeling. While they progress through Piaget's stages in the same manner as other children, their progression appears to be accelerated, and, in addition, their thought processes within a stage of development are significantly more complex.

Young gifted children develop and grow through the same physical, emotional, and intellectual stages as other children. Therefore, they may encounter some of the same difficulties in communicating and understanding the world. Yet, I have come to believe that gifted children bring a different and unique dimension of thinking to the way in which they cope with life.

Jean Piaget's (1952; 1955) theory of the development of the child's thought processes generally has been recognized as the basic theory of intellectual development. Piaget believes that the child approaches life with an underdeveloped thinking apparatus and, therefore, will often misinterpret the world and the adults around him.

I would like to begin with a brief summary of some of Piaget's major concepts. According to Piaget (1964; Piaget & Inhelder, 1964), the following methods of thinking are prerequisites for adult thought: *multiple classification, seriation, reversibility,* and *conservation.*

Multiple Classification

To understand the world, we must realize that things, people and ideas can be simultaneously classified in more than one way. A woman can be a mother, daughter, sister, and teacher, all at the same time. A young child, who is in what Piaget calls the *preoperational stage*, can classify only according to a single criterion (e.g., a mother can only be a mother). Imagine how this child feels when his mother goes out and becomes a teacher. He feels that he has lost her, for within the constraints of his ability to think and reason, she is no longer a mother.

This helps to explain why a three-year-old child might go off to school happily, then suddenly refuse to attend, even though nothing at school has changed. The only change was that his mother had taken a teaching job. Previously, he felt safe knowing that Mother was being Mother at home—even while he went to school. But when she became a teacher, she stopped being a mother for him.

This was a loss of security and stability, both intellectually and emotionally, for the young child. He felt as though suddenly he had no support. A situation like that can be understood if one is aware of infantile thought processes. Through many experiences and processes, the child learns the concept of multiple classification and can then, of course, deal with a situation like this one in a much more realistic manner.

Seriation

To understand the fact of learning, of change, of growth and development, we must understand the concept of seriation. Seriation means that things can be ordered from less to more according to a common property, such as size. The concept of multiple classification is necessary to an understanding of seriation. This means that we understand that things can change gradually, that you can be big and little at the same time (bigger than your sister but smaller than your father). A child in the preoperational stage cannot grasp this. From this level of development, you are either big or little, and no change is possible. You are either good or bad. The very young child, when scolded, feels that he is bad. Again, in knowing these thought processes, we can better understand the emotions of a young child.

Reversibility

The concept of reversibility means that things can return to their original condition if nothing has been changed in their basic state. For example, an upside down table is still a table, even though we may use it like a boat. Or, using the previous example, my mother is still my mother, even though she leaves the house and teaches. Reversibility is essential to understanding mathematical relations: how addition is related to subtraction, and multiplication is related to division. For example, five plus three equals eight; therefore, eight minus three equals five. If the child does not have the concept of reversibility, the fact that five plus three equals eight does not bear any relationship to what eight minus three might be. It does not give the child a clue to the answer.

Conservation

The above concepts are prerequisites for the concept of conservation. Conservation can be thought of as the ability to think in abstract terms. It marks the beginning of the operational stage. Conservation can be defined as the cognition that certain properties, such as quantity, weight, volume, etc., remain invariant. That means they are conserved in the face of certain transformation. Examples of this concept are displaying objects or object parts in space, sectioning an object into pieces, and changing shapes.

For example, quantity does not change, even though the form in which it appears does change. A piece of paper crumpled up contains the same amount of paper as before it was crumpled. This concept can be tested by the famous Coca-Cola experiment. One takes two bottles of Coke, shows them to the child, and asks if there is the same amount of Coke in each bottle. When the child says yes, one is poured into a thin, tall glass and the other into a wide, shallow glass. The child is then asked again if there is the same amount of Coke in each glass. If the child is not able to conserve, she will be deceived by the appearance and will believe there is more Coke in the tall glass. If she can tell that the amount is the same because she saw where it originally came from, that means that she has an abstract, operational way of thinking: She can conserve.

As was stated in the beginning, all children go through all these stages. There are no exceptions. Some may pass through them faster than others, some may begin them earlier, but all have to go through the process, including the gifted child. Gifted children may understand certain factors more easily and faster, but they do follow the same pattern.

I did not always believe this, for I have long been aware of the difference in reactions to the world by the gifted child; yet my own research proved this to be true. Nevertheless, my observations and deductions from these observations remain unchanged over the years. The following is an attempt to integrate these seemingly contradictory conclusions.

In 1965, I conducted a study with Dr. Irving Sigel (a Piagetian researcher), then associated with the Merrill Palmer Institute in Detroit, of the conceptual development of gifted children at our school using Piaget's theory (Roeper & Sigel, 1966; Sigel, Roeper, & Hooper, 1966). One of the purposes of our study was to determine whether the ability to conserve could be produced by training the children in the prerequisite skills of multiple classification, reversibility and seriation. Previous research attempting to teach young children to conserve had been unsuccessful (Flavell, 1963). Our sample consisted of two groups of gifted students ranging in age from 4 years 9 months to 5 years 1 month. One group was trained on the prerequisite skills and the other, the control group, was not. The mean IQs for the two groups were similar: 149 for the trained group, and 152 for the control group.

The method used for training was the inquiry method. The children were not simply informed of a concept, but were guided to discover it themselves through observation and discussion. The three abstract ideas described by Piaget were introduced through examples. Each process was shown and discussed by different methods until the children's comments reflected a real understanding. Where the children seemed to have grasped the idea in a specific context, other situations were introduced, and finally they were led into generalizing their newly found understanding. Verbalizing, according to Jerome Bruner (1960), can protect the child against being overwhelmed by superficial and erroneous evidence. In other words, the discussion itself helps the child to acquire the ability to conserve.

The control group and the training group were both tested on various facets of conservation. The training group did considerably better than the control group on the post-training tasks of conservation of substance, weight and volume. Only one of the seven children in the control group improved her ability to conserve, but she had been able to conserve solid and liquid substances in the pretest. All but one of the nine children in the training group gained in their conceptions of conservation. These findings were important because they showed that appropriate teaching of prerequisite skills could improve children's abilities to conserve. It is possible that these children's high levels of giftedness, perhaps indicating different thought processes, enabled us to teach them conservation concepts that could not be taught to children in previous studies. The results are also important because they demonstrated that gifted children could acquire complex concepts of conservation considerably earlier than Piaget (1964) had suggested was possible. According to Piaget, conservation appears between the ages of eight and twelve. While they were able to accomplish the tasks at an earlier age, gifted children still had to go through the same cognitive developmental stages: Certain concepts are necessary prerequisites for others.

How do we explain that observers all around the world discover gifted children because they are impressed with their specific thinking ability even at the preoperational level? I am saying that gifted children think like others and yet they do not. How do we solve this seeming contradiction? By not considering it a contradiction!

I think the gifted child goes through the same developmental phases, but functions *within each phase* in his or her own specific mode of thinking. In fact, these children even use their lack of having attained a certain developmental stage to widen their horizons and creativity of thought.

For example, all children, whether or not they were part of the study, had a great interest in outer space at that time, for the first rockets had been launched. They had a realistic understanding of weightlessness and its consequences. I can recall their delightful stories of what happens in a rocket during its flight in space. The children also understood that things which are outside the earth's gravity do not automatically return. In addition, they recognized the concept of "being in orbit." Most of these children were not yet of the age where they understood reversibility. They had not learned that what goes up must come down. Staying in orbit, therefore, was no problem. Their understanding of a three-stage rocket and how it had to leave the earth's gravity and all that it entailed, however, was very sophisticated.

Another example is the young gifted child who becomes excited with the idea that the world is round and understands that the Chinese live on the other side of the world before she can understand the concept of multiple classification. This same child could not understand that you can live on Woodward Avenue, in Detroit, in Michigan, in the United States, and still live in one spot. She had, according to her developmental stage, no problem in understanding that two people can live in two places, each in their own place: one in America and one in China. This is similar to the concept that there are mothers and there are teachers. That, too, is understandable, as long as the mother and the teacher are not the same person.

Here is a third example. A little girl, four years old, told me that she wanted to live on the moon. When I asked her why, she replied, "Because I'm a dancer." And when I asked her why it is better to be a dancer on the moon than on the earth, she answered, "You weigh less on the moon and so it will be easier for you to dance." She had been told that dancing would be easier if she weighed less. She understood the concept of "more and less" but not that of seriation at the time (i.e., that she weighs more than some and less than others). She also did not know about the principle of conservation and, therefore, would find nothing wrong with the idea that you may weigh one amount in one place and something else somewhere else without adding or taking away any pounds. In other words, her lack of ability to conserve made it possible for her to develop this idea. She had an IQ over 170, and I truly believe that another child with less intelligence would not have come up with this very ingenious solution to her weight problem.

All of the above serves to support the paradox that gifted children are in many ways like other children, but there also exists a basic difference in the *quality* of their thinking and feeling. While they progress through Piaget's stages in the same manner as other children, their progression appears to be accelerated, and, in addition, their thought processes within a stage of development are significantly more complex. My thoughts about the ways in which the gifted differ come from extensive observation over a long period of time. We still have much more to learn about the ways in which gifted children differ from others in their intellectual development. I hope this paper might stimulate further dialogue and research on this question.

References

Bruner, J.S. *The Process of Education*. Cambridge, MA: Harvard University Press, 1960.

Flavell, J.H. *The Developmental Psychology of Jean Piaget*. Princeton, NJ: Van Nostrand, 1963.

Piaget, J. *The Origins of Intelligence in the Child*. New York: International Universities Press, 1952.

—*The Language and Thought of the Child*. New York: World, 1955.

—*The Child's Conception of Numbers* (3rd ed.). London: Routledge & Kegan Paul, 1964.

—& Inhelder, B. *The Early Growth of Logic in the Child*. New York: Harper & Row, 1964.

Roeper, A., & Sigel, I.E. "Finding the Clue to Children's Thought Processes." *Young Children*, Vol. XXI, No. 6 (September, 1966), pp. 335-348. Also published as a chapter in Hartup, W.W., & Smotheregill (Eds.). *The Young Child: Review of Research*. Washington, DC: National Association for the Education of Young Children, 1967, pp. 77–95.

—Hooper, F.H., & Sigel, I.E. "A Training Procedure for Acquisition of Piaget's Conservation of Quantity: A Pilot Study and Its Replication." *British Journal of Educational Psychology*, 36 (3), pp. 301–311 (1966). This article was declared a "classic" by the *Social Sciences Citation Index (SSCI)* in February, 1986, since it had been cited in over 50 publications, making it the most cited paper ever published in the *British Journal of Educational Psychology*.

The Teaching and Learning of Reading: A Personal Statement on a Most Controversial Subject

Published in *Parent Communication*, vol. 9, no. 3 (Spring, 1976), pp. 1–3.

I have often heard it said that "if a child knows how to read, everything else falls into place." I disagree. Children do not learn to read until they are ready and when they feel accepted as whole persons. Therefore, reading is not a priority in itself. The development of the total person must remain the ultimate priority.

In the area of education, no subject matter is as hotly debated as that of reading. Millions of dollars are spent annually for research on the learning process. Thousands of books have been written on the subject, and reading is talked about whenever educators get together. Over the last 30 years, I have seen the pendulum swing back and forth concerning opinions about how reading is learned and when it is learned, as well as how to teach, what to teach, when to teach, and even where to teach it. We have tried individualized education, self-contained classrooms, ability grouping, peer teaching, open classrooms, and traditional classrooms, but the debate about reading has not changed in context or in intensity. No agreement has been reached, and the issues remain emotional ones for all concerned—educators, parents, and especially children. The reason for this is easy to understand. The ability to read is a most necessary tool for participation in modern world society.

I would like to share with you my thoughts and position regarding the teaching of reading. I find it more comfortable to speak for myself only, even though I believe there is some general agreement, as well as some differences, among the staff at our school. Also, I am very aware of the responsibility of speaking for others because, to my amazement, others have often spoken for me and have told me what "my opinions are."

For example, during the early years of the school, when we had a regular nursery, kindergarten, and elementary grades, it happened more than once that parents would "confess" to me that they had taught their four-year-old to read. They knew, they said, that it was against our principles. Did I think they had done some irreparable harm? They made an assumption based on general attitudes that existed during that period of time. In reality, there has never been a time when I did not believe that a child's readiness to learn was based on his or her developmental growth and not on age. In fact, I had often seen to it in those days that particular children were given the opportunity to learn to read in our nursery school and kindergarten.

I also remember the veritable storm of disagreement among early childhood educators when we introduced reading at our school on a more widespread basis for three-, four-, and five-year-olds. They assumed that I believed *all* pre-school children should learn how to read. And they accused me of pressuring young children, robbing them of their childhood. Some people literally would not speak to me. Today, some people tell me that I give low priority to the learning of reading!

I would, therefore, like to state my position as clearly as possible. My experiences during the past 30 years have only served to confirm my belief that age and developmental phases are not interchangeable. A three-year-old may read and be eager to read. We would be remiss in not offering that child the opportunity to do so. A six-year-old, on the other hand, may be neither ready nor eager to read. In this case, we might harm that child by forcing him to learn. Both children end up with a lack of skills and interest or develop other emotional reactions if adults are not sensitive to their developmental rhythms. However, through natural maturation, more six-year-olds are ready to read than three-year-olds. At the older age, we must be watchful for any reasons unrelated to development that might keep a child from learning to read. At the younger age of three, we should watch for similar signals which might predict difficulties with reading in the future.

Reading has always been at the center of my life, for it is one of my greatest sources of pleasure as well as learning. To help young people unlock the secrets of the printed word is a goal that is well integrated in my general philosophy of education. And it is because I hold the whole concept of reading in such high regard that I feel it must be handled with the greatest of care. Yet the skill of reading is not all that is involved in learning to read. We must simultaneously open other doors of the world for the child—the doors to poetry and prose, to history and science, to other cultures and countries, and to various experiences. The acquisition of reading is an integral part of the development of the whole person. We cannot separate the growth of the whole person from the development of individual skills. They are part of the whole, and all either enhance each other or disturb each other.

The above concept may be where my point of view differs from that of others. Whether in practice only or in theory, the learning and teaching of reading is often "lifted out" of the concern for the rest of the person and treated as something separate. Often it becomes the only concern, with everything else receding into the background. Time and thought are spent on areas outside reading only after specific reading skills have been covered. I believe that all areas are so completely intertwined that they should never be separated from each other. This does not mean that reading or other skills should not be taught separately to some extent. But we must always see that learning to read is integrated into the whole personality.

I have often heard it said that "if a child knows how to read, everything else falls into place." I disagree. Children do not learn to read until they are ready and when they feel accepted as whole persons. Therefore, reading is not a priority in itself. The development of the total person must remain the ultimate priority. However, to help this growth, there are times in a child's life when special emphasis on the learning and teaching of reading is appropriate and absolutely necessary. Since personal growth and development is an individual matter, I believe that learning to read, as with other skills, is something that is completely individual. Both the teaching and the expectations must be geared to the individual and not tied to an arbitrary norm.

I realize that these expectations can lead to a dilemma. We live in a society where we look at the individual in relation to society. We question how the particular individual will meet the conditions he or she is exposed to in the world. The resolution of this dilemma has led to the development of the tyranny of the standardized test. Experience has shown that success on these tests does not necessarily predict well-integrated, successful, and happy lives. These tests are the reason why so many have separated specific measurable skills from the person and have forgotten the rest of the person. It can be documented that standardized tests have led to much personal failure and have produced no outstanding success in reading skills. Still, I am not against the use of standardized tests as diagnostic tools, as long as we never forget their limitations or allow them to exploit us. The tests do give us certain information that may be very helpful for the individual. Furthermore, the human mind needs guidelines to orient its thoughts and actions and understanding.

In all education, we are confronted with a two-pronged task. We have to help the child grow best in relation to self as well as in relation to society. The child is only a truly integrated human being if we succeed in both. Our educational procedures, therefore, must be based on this double task. The environment, other people—children and adults, and the atmosphere in which a child lives—have an enormous impact on a child's attitude toward reading. If we accept the necessity of thinking of the individual within the context of his or her surroundings, let us examine those general life conditions, both at home and at school, which would best promote the ability to read.

Children will always know the value of words if they grow up in an environment where conversation is considered a joy and an art as well as a means of communication and growth, where conversation is used as a way to express feelings as well as thoughts, and where children are included in this speech community. Children will take for granted that reading is a necessity of life if they grow up in an environment where there are books, magazines, a gathering of information, and other mental stimulation that are as much a part of daily life as television.

As Maria Montessori (1936) pointed out many years ago, there is a sensitive period in the development of a child when he or she is just ready to learn. The adults in the environment need to be aware of this golden moment in each child, for to react too late or too early may be detrimental. In order to want to learn, the child must feel strong motivation to do so. The type of environment described above often serves as strong motivation. A child will want to learn to read, not in order to pass a test or to do better than others, but because he or she needs the skill in order to master life. The motivation becomes the child's property, as does the skill, rather than belonging to external sources such as parents and teachers. Once this basis of self-motivation is established, a child will be further motivated by living up to the expectations of the adults, their standards, and their examples.

An important aspect of creating a favorable atmosphere for children to learn to read relates to expectations. These must be realistic in terms of the particular stage each child is going through. Parents and teachers must be in agreement with each other, and the children must also know what they expect and what they can realistically expect of themselves. If expectations are out of reach, it will be detrimental, just as is the case when expectations are too low. If our expectations for children are realistic, we will be aware of the time and manner in which specific emphasis on reading must be created within a generally stimulating environment. At this point, the teacher must find a particular structure and method which will fit the particular needs of each child or, at times, groups of children.

There are certain characteristics among gifted children that require particular responses from adults. Many gifted children, of course, are self-taught readers. In these cases, we need to understand how a particular child learns, because there have been instances where our methods of instruction have been counter to the child's learning style and to the methods which have proven successful for a particular child. With gifted children who are not self-taught readers, it becomes important to surround them with stimulation and experiences to show them that reading is going to open new doors of learning. Some gifted children do not find the mechanics of reading exciting because their intellectual capacity and range of interests are so far beyond the kind of subject matter found in early readers. In these cases, it is important to use the children's intelligence to make it clear that they need reading as an absolutely necessary tool for life.

What are some factors that help children to develop the skills and motivation for reading?

- An atmosphere which creates a good self-image.
- An atmosphere which provides safety and security so that the child's energies can be directed toward growth rather than toward emotional and physical self-preservation.
- Adults who are able to provide this atmosphere.
- The right to trial-and-error.
- Respect for a child's own learning style, plus teachers who are able to adapt to the particular child's learning style or who can recognize the fact that they are not able to adapt to it and will find another adult who is.
- Time and emphasis on direct teaching of reading to individuals and small groups.
- Mutual motivation by peers or older children.
- A positive, realistic appraisal of where the child stands in terms of reading.
- Recognition of factors which interfere with a child's learning to read and consideration of them in our plans.

Children who are at risk for difficulties learning to read may suffer from one or more of the following problems:

- Preoccupation with their own fantasies, their own inner life, at the expense of their schoolwork.
- Chronic physical problems, such as allergies, etc.
- Stressful situations, such as divorce or death of a loved one.
- Low self-image.
- Feelings that they will never do as well as older siblings or that they are not expected to do as well (e.g., girls vs. boys).

- Paralyzing perfectionism; afraid to try for fear that they will not be perfect. Not being perfect means being a failure.

- Fear of being unable to live up to expectations of adults in their environment.

- Excessive competitiveness; afraid that they will not be the best in the class or do as well as their peers.

- The absence of proper help or opportunity.

- Pressure to read when they are not developmentally ready.

- Parents who show no interest in their achievements.

- Perceptual problems or other learning disabilities.

A specific task of parents and teachers is to recognize such interference with normal development, through observation, interview, or diagnostic testing. Once the problems are recognized, a plan of action needs to be devised with the child, and expectations must be revised. At that point, it is important to include in one's expectations different timing and a trust in the future. I have seen children who could not learn how to read until age nine or ten and then made great strides. I know of others who only came into their own in high school and then made up for lost time, doing better than others.

There is an enormous number of specific methods of teaching reading and improving a child's specific reading skills. Some children are more able to use one method than others. Some teachers prefer certain methods over others. Almost all methods are valid for individual children at different times.

There are a great many activities that do not seem to be directly related to reading but which, nevertheless, are important foundations for the reading process. Some people might think that spending school time on these "frivolous" activities detracts from the serious business of learning how to read. However, they teach skills that are basic to reading and stimulate the child's desire to learn to read. For example, creating interests in different fields will motivate the child to want to read. This could be any area of interest ranging from baseball to science, from Superman to social studies—whatever may excite the child. Stimulation by the librarian is of utmost importance for this. Physical education, dance, music, and art cannot be underestimated in their importance in helping the child learn how to deal with the printed word. These activities help develop spatial perception, eye-hand coordination, appreciation of one's body in space, etc. All these daily experiences can be used very consciously and thoughtfully in terms of providing a basis for a child's learning how to read. One of the many tasks of the teacher, therefore, is to balance all these experiences for each individual, considering not only the mastery of reading, but also the best opportunities for acquisition of other skills and the child's overall growth.

What does all this mean in terms of the teaching of reading at Roeper City and Country School? The philosophy of reading expressed above is a radical departure from the traditional approach to the teaching of reading.

In the past, the structure of teaching, the diagnosis, and the motivation used to be very well-defined. At three years you played, at six you learned how to read. From then on, at the end of each school year, a specific goal had to be reached by all children. If you went beyond this goal as a child, you were ahead. If you did not reach this goal, you were behind, according to the standards set up by society. This was decided by tests. Most of the day in first grade was spent on activities directly related to reading. Instruction usually took place in three groups, dividing children by reading ability: the good ones, the middle ones, and the bad ones. Motivation was managed by marks and remarks.

For us, and many others like us, this whole framework became very uncomfortable. It seemed artificial and unrealistic, and we could not live with it anymore. We had to create a new framework and learn to live within it. We had to find ways which would tell us about the individual child's learning style, the individual child's motivation, the individual child's growth pattern, and the individual child's whole personality. We had to find ways to relate the individual child to the demands of society. We had to find ways to create some new general guidelines to use as a framework without letting it dictate to us. We had to find out which of the old to discard and which to use. It was a real pioneering effort, like discovering a new country and familiarizing ourselves with it. Children and parents became part of this effort, for only with their cooperation and much trust could we venture into this new territory.

It was not always easy during the last few years. There were times of discouragement as well as times of enthusiasm. Every step of the way we became more familiar, we learned new skills partially through our own experience, partially through workshops, books, etc. It was also exciting to see different kinds of growth in many of the children, different from what we used to see under the old structure. We watched carefully all during this time to see where we might have erred and tried to remedy it.

Now we are becoming more and more familiar and comfortable with our new structure, and it would be generalized like this: There are certain very broad developmental stages where certain skills in general can be expected. They are somewhat related to age. We have formulated these and are in the process of refining them and defining more specific expectations for each stage. Children at certain ages have much in common but are basically individuals with individual needs. Our diversity in classroom structure, depending on the teacher's personality, allows for the diversity of children's needs on each level. Within each classroom, the teacher plans for the needs of each individual child. Tests are used for diagnostic purposes whenever indicated. We go through a very careful process of placing the child into a group and with a teacher who fulfills the child's particular needs. Parents and children participate in the placement process. Reading is of central interest to each teacher, and each teacher determines the methods appropriate for his or her group of children.

Reference

Montessori, M. *The Secret of Childhood.* London: Longmans Green, 1936.

How to Help the Underachieving Gifted Child

Published in *Parents' Press* (October, 1992), pp. 15–16.

In my opinion and experience, in most cases the problem is not in the child, but rather in the child's school interaction. The child may be in a situation where the academic expectations are not geared toward the needs of gifted children and are not in tune with the way they function, learn, and feel.

Seven-year-old Lisa's parents worked very hard to find the best school for their gifted child, and they felt confident in the one they decided upon. Lisa's teacher is friendly and runs a relaxed, flexible, interesting classroom. But something has changed between Lisa and her parents. Every day after school, there are fights over homework.

"It will only take you a few minutes to do it, Lisa," they remind her. Lisa's face reddens, she begins sobbing, and she runs to her room. Only on weekends is Lisa her usual smiling self.

"The homework is so dull! I've done those subtractions for two years. Why do I have to do two boring pages of the same old thing?" Lisa wails.

"The teacher wants everyone to do it," her father says.

"You make me do it just because the teacher says so. You just obey the teacher," Lisa cries. "I feel so alone!"

Lisa's parents look at each other in astonishment. She is right, they realize. In a strange way, they *have* abandoned their child.

Most of the children I see in my consultation service for the gifted are, like Lisa, about seven or eight years old. Their parents come because there is trouble at school. My child is a dreamer, they say. My child has problems paying attention. My child is the class clown. My child talks too much. My child throws paper. My child makes too much noise. The problem started when my child entered grade school. What mistakes have I made? Something is wrong with my child!

Something *is* wrong, but not necessarily with the child.

Confronted with labels like "underachiever" or "problem child," gifted children and their parents are left feeling confused, frightened, and guilt-ridden. The parents are sometimes told—often mistakenly—that their child may have dyslexia, attention deficit disorder, behavioral problems, or a host of other difficulties, including being immature.

The child may fail in class or refuse to do homework, may not pay attention, or may disrupt the class. The child may be a loner or may have run-ins with other children. The parents are told to seek counseling or tutoring for the child or parenting classes for themselves. To the child, it seems that everyone—the teachers, the principal, the parents—is looking and speaking about all this with great seriousness and holding many conferences. It all looks grave and threatening to the child, who begins to feel like a failure, feels misunderstood or angry, and is at a loss to please parents and educators. Parents, too, may feel that they have failed. They may feel disappointed in or angry with their child, and may find themselves supervising or disciplining the child more strictly.

Such situations, of course, are not unique to children who have been formally identified as gifted. Individual learning styles among children do not always coincide with general academic expectations, and many children and their parents will confront the "underachiever" and "problem child" labels. While these situations seem to occur more frequently and visibly among gifted children, the concerns and possible solutions can often apply to other children as well.

There are many cases in which concerns about a particular child are both obvious and justified. In many other situations, however, I have come across curious contradictions:

- A child is seen as having a short attention span and being disruptive, but in his after-school class at the University of California science building he is able to concentrate totally. He receives a D in science at school while working on complex experiments at home.

- Because she is deemed "immature" and unready for the academic challenge of first grade, a kindergartner is being held back. At the same time, she outwits her father in a game of chess.

- A child does not pay attention in school. Instead, she daydreams about how to save rain forests. Her parents report that her knowledge of the complex interdependencies of ecological life cycles is remarkable, but she is not rewarded at school.

- A child does outstanding work in second, fourth, and sixth grades, but curiously enough, fails first, third, and fifth.

- A teacher is concerned because a seven-year-old child never counts correctly at school, yet knows how to multiply and divide correctly at home.

- A fifth-grader is considered slow but, unknown to his teacher, he writes beautiful poetry.

- One child acts up in class and the other never participates, but both do outstanding work in a summer course in math for the gifted.

Many of these children are clearly aware of their difficulties and discuss them openly with me. Often they say that they expected school to be different. They have so many questions for which they had hoped to find answers in school. They feel that their teachers and classmates do not understand them. In most cases, they cannot explain why they are in trouble. Many underachieving gifted children believe that something must be wrong with them—if the teachers think so, it must be true—but they do not know what is wrong or what to do about it.

Many of these children go to good schools and have dedicated teachers who sincerely want to help. A concerned teacher may believe that the child has a problem in need of a remedy when, in reality, the characteristics of the child and the general expectations of the educational community do not match.

It is this mismatch that is commonly interpreted as a "problem" belonging to the child. In my opinion and experience, in most cases the problem is not in the child, but rather in the child's school interaction. The child may be in a situation where the academic expectations are not geared toward the needs of gifted children and are not in tune with the way they function, learn, and feel. These expectations originate from the traditional concept of achievement: the learning of skills by following a prescribed, sequential course of study.

All gifted children are expected and assumed to excel in traditional achievements. However, many gifted children bring to their educations a set of characteristics different from the norm:

- Gifted children are concept learners rather than skill learners, and they often have their own interests.

- Gifted children do not necessarily learn sequentially.

- Some gifted children are perfectionists.

- Gifted children are global learners who may learn the large concepts while neglecting the details.

Because of these characteristics, certain gifted children require a broader definition of what exactly constitutes achievement. It is often mistakenly believed that all gifted children learn traditional subjects faster and better than other children. In reality, gifted children sometimes learn to read late, do not necessarily compute math problems well, may be dreadful at spelling, and often do not have good handwriting—all of which are rote skills stressed in elementary school. These same children long for more conceptual information in science, math, literature, or philosophy. Other gifted children may function on a higher skill level than average, but they are not allowed to proceed at their own accelerated pace.

This is where problems can arise. Frustrated gifted children may become restless and talk to their neighbors or sail the proverbial paper airplane. Those who are perfectionists and who do not quite understand that many people learn by trial-and-error may fail because they do not want to risk something unless they can be sure the results will be perfect. Many other gifted children feel excluded by their classmates, who may not understand them.

How to Help

When a child does not produce what a teacher expects, he is seen as an underachiever. From the child's point of view, his education is not helping him to find the answers he seeks. The traditional structure of education may feel like stricture to the gifted child. Out of this mutual disappointment grow the difficulties.

The child is often unable to define his reactions or to describe his side of the picture. The parents hear only the impressions of the teachers, and they draw conclusions from this single point of view. Parents often still react to their child's teacher with the same awe they experienced as school children, and often they do not question the school's judgment, even though many teachers do not have much background in understanding the educational needs of gifted children and thus judge these youngsters as they do other children.

Giftedness is a process, not a product. Gifted children feel and think differently from others. They are more concerned with the *why* than the *how* of learning. For example, learning why a bicycle does not fall down when it is ridden may be of greater interest to a gifted child than actually learning to ride a bike. Educational achievement, for a gifted child, lies in understanding the reason the bike stays up. Similarly, many gifted children are substantially ahead in learning math concepts while lagging behind in the ability to do computations. In a learning environment where only computational skills are valued, a gifted child may soon be considered an underachiever.

For these reasons, it is important for parents and teachers to look at the whole situation and not to assume automatically that the problem lies with the child. The danger is that the parents may begin to see the child as flawed, while the child may see the school as flawed and feel that her parents have become spokespersons for the school. It is absolutely necessary that the child receive her parents' support and their promise to help. The child must feel that her parents and, hope-fully, the school are on her side and that they will evaluate the situation as carefully as possible from all points of view.

How can parents show this support? Let us return to Lisa and what happened before her parents understood her particular needs.

The nightly battles over homework escalated, and Lisa became more and more rebellious. Her parents felt obliged to withdraw one privilege after another as a means of convincing Lisa to do her homework. Home life became entirely disrupted, revolving as it did around the nightly homework battles.

When I asked Lisa's parents if they felt that Lisa's homework was contributing positively toward her educational growth, they both admit-ted that Lisa found the homework boring. There was no doubt that Lisa knew the material. The only benefit of doing it, in their opinion, was that Lisa would learn to complete unpleasant tasks, which everyone has to learn eventually.

I asked the parents if they had admitted to Lisa that they knew the homework was boring for her. No, they said, that would only be support-ing her rebelliousness. The parents followed my advice to share their own reactions with Lisa, who immediately felt relieved because she felt understood. Her parents then explained that she had no choice but to do the unpleasant task of homework, but they promised to find a way to help her. Keeping their promise, the parents held a joint meeting with the principal and Lisa's teacher. They explained Lisa's particular needs in a manner that demonstrated their understanding of the point of view of the school, which had to accommodate children with all sorts of learn-ing styles and needs. An agreement was reached that Lisa would not be given homework assignments for material she had already mastered. The meeting produced another benefit: In-service training covering the educational needs of gifted children was introduced at the school.

In situations where this sort of cooperation between parents and the school cannot be achieved, it might prove necessary to change the child's learning environment by finding another school. This does not mean that I advocate allowing the child to dominate the situation. There are occasions when children try to avoid *necessary* tasks, and in such cases they need to be expected to complete school assignments. However, the most important point I would like to make is that a child should never feel left alone to cope with problems. This is true whether the problems result from learning disabilities or emotional difficulties, or whether the problems grow out of an educational mismatch. Parental support is the basis of a child's sense of security. Because it is important to view the situation both realistically and from all points of view, it may be helpful to seek professional advice.

The Young Gifted Girl:
A Contemporary View

Presented as part of a panel symposium, "Creativity, Magic and Morality," at the 54th annual meeting of the American Orthopsychiatric Association, San Francisco, California (March, 1978). Subsequently published in *The Roeper Review* (1978).

While society is beginning to accept the rights of women and the rights of the gifted, it is devaluating and often ignoring the rights of children. What the gifted girl has gained on one side, she is losing on the other.

The civil rights movement of the 1950s and 1960s, originally born as a protest against the oppressed status of blacks, had a liberating effect on many other groups. Two of the movements spawned by the new awareness of basic human rights had a deep and to some extent unexpected impact on the gifted girl. The modern gifted girl is a psychologically different person than her gifted ancestors. She has gone through a series of changes and is still in the middle of a very fundamental one. These changes relate to the manner in which the gifted girl is seen by society and how she herself reacts to this perception.

During the days when sex roles were rigidly defined, few gifted girls were able to surface, to be recognized by themselves and others as gifted. There were, of course, some whose talents and innate drives could not be suppressed, and they gained acceptance in the world as the "exceptions" in areas such as literature, music, or other fields that were traditionally reserved for men. Women, other than these exceptions, could grow in the limited areas that were reserved for their sex, such as motherhood, a teaching career, a nursing career, and others. These areas then were automatically relegated to a lower status, and although the rewards of recognition could be forthcoming, they still remained behind the sex barrier. What did this mean for the gifted girl whose giftedness was working inside of her, pushing her and making her dissatisfied with her fate, yet finding the doors to fulfillment hermetically closed?

The following phenomenon used to be noticed by many educators of young children and observers of adults. Young boys were usually active and outgoing. They were, after an initial head start by girls in the early grades, the high achievers and the award winners. They also were the troublemakers and, often, the underachievers. Girls were passive, obedient, wanted to be pretty, at times were catty, and, as a rule, accepted their assigned role without protest. Boys in trouble usually outnumbered girls in that category by a large number. On the other hand, it was observed that adult women far outnumbered men in mental hospitals.

I believe that many of the boys in trouble and many of the women in mental hospitals were and are gifted. Since my subject is the gifted girl, I do not want to go deeply into the reasons why gifted boys are often in trouble. I would like to say only that I think boys were raised to be active, to express their feelings, and to be aggressive. On the other hand, they also felt oppressed in certain ways. They had an enormous burden of expectations laid upon them by society and often by their families, especially if they were known as being particularly capable in certain areas. Why did young gifted girls accept their assigned roles and often only in later years react with unhappiness or even mental illness?

One of the characteristics typical of the gifted is their enormous awareness of the complexities and dangers of the world. For this reason, gifted people are often not spontaneously daring; they cannot be certain about that to which they are being exposed. It is for this reason that we find gifted children at times to be particularly infantile. They may try to postpone accepting the responsibilities that come with growing older. This often creates initial passivity. The young girl is, or rather was, required to be passive and obedient and to cater to the expectations of her environment. She lived within a very well-defined framework, and this offered protection. Inside of this framework her mother was very visible as a model to emulate. The girl received love and support from her father and gratification as appropriate for her young needs as long as she stayed within the prescribed limits. In other words, it was just because she was gifted that she appreciated the safety of the early years that existed for the typical girl. Her giftedness also helped her develop the skills to fit the image of the girl—a certain helplessness coupled with helpfulness that appealed to the assumed superior ability of men. She relished the praise she received for serving others, for giving of herself, and she consciously developed her charms and beauty. She moved from the protection of her father into the protection of her husband. She felt safe. Later, she threw herself into her career as a mother. In fact, she often became a possessive mother, for this was the only avenue by which she could fulfill herself. She lived through her children. Eventually, however, she lapsed into depression when her children left and she found that she had not been allowed to develop herself in directions other than the one accepted by society. It was at this time that she often became dissatisfied with her role as a mother as well as a wife, and problems became evident.

What happened to gifted women at the time when society became aware of the fact of giftedness in human beings? Did this change their status? I am afraid that it did not bring about a basic change in the way the gifted woman saw herself and was seen by society.

One of the several waves of interest in the gifted appeared around the second half of the 1950s. This particular movement was not one of liberation. For most people, it was defined in utilitarian terms. The gifted were considered a national resource and, as such, society was mostly interested in the product that became possible by the ability of gifted people. Society became interested in those aspects of giftedness that were quantitatively measurable. This meant that the gifted child who was better, faster, and more able to produce was recognized. It was a very limited definition of giftedness, and if a child had these characteristics, they were considered the property of society, not of the child.

Nevertheless, this new emphasis opened doors that had been closed and provided practical and financial opportunities and recognition to all economic groups of gifted children, not only for those who could afford special schools. But almost by definition, giftedness was to a great extent restricted to men. One looked for the kind of product that had been traditionally part of the male world: technology. After all, it was the event of *Sputnik* that sparked the interest in the gifted child.

Yet proud mothers and fathers began to identify their gifted children—for the most part, boys. Girls, by definition, were not supposed to be gifted. The stereotype of what constituted femininity left little chance for a girl to be classified as gifted. Those girls who were gifted were told that they had the mind of a boy.

This tendency was borne out by the applications at the Roeper City and Country School for gifted children during the 1950s and 1960s. Usually about two-thirds boys and one-third girls applied to be enrolled in our school. The definition of a feminine girl and that of giftedness seemed to be mutually exclusive. In fact, at this point the gifted girl had a double problem. Society was slow to recognize the gifted, but when it did, the door opened for the boy while the girl sat by and watched him go through. The gifted girl was left with her femininity. If she dared to be gifted, a negative label would be put on her and she would be seen as a "bluestocking" by society.

This was particularly true if there was both a brother and a sister in the home. If the brother had beautiful curly hair and the girl was outstanding in math, they both suffered. Some of the stereotyped reactions included, "She's an aggressive female," or "Are you going to let a girl beat you?," or "Of course, it's my bad luck to have a curly-headed boy and a girl who reads all day instead of helping me in the kitchen," or "Men don't marry girls who are brighter than they are." The girl's talent became a handicap; she was not supposed to be that which she could not help but be. The father would often become resentful if the girl competed with her brother in any way. The brother felt inferior and hostile if the sister developed her talents. The brother was supposed to be competitive, but the sister, on the other hand, had little support if she excelled. In such a situation, often neither the boy nor the girl got the necessary support or recognition. They both disappointed their parents.

The real milestone in the history of the gifted girl was the advent of the women's movement. Women, especially gifted women, began to struggle against their traditional role and develop a new image and concept of womanhood. This movement was soon followed by a renewed interest in the gifted child. This time, both concepts were based on the civil rights model. The gifted person was no longer viewed as a resource, but had a civil right to the opportunity to develop his or her personality to the fullest. Giftedness was not defined in quantitative terms, but was seen as a different personality structure based on affective as well as cognitive differences that functioned through both conscious and unconscious processes.

Now the world had opened its doors to women. Women had the recognized rights and abilities to go in any direction they chose. And here they stood, looking at the complex landscape for the first time. How were they going to deal with it? They had no tradition, no skills, and no support system to go where they now had a right to go. Tradition, skills, and support were still all in the hands of men.

New opportunities, along with new problems, appeared for the gifted girl. Where was she going to look for a model? To her mother? If the young preschool child or even the adolescent looks at her mother, she sees her mother floundering, trying to cope with a terrifying course. And if this mother in turn looks at her own mother, she finds no fulfillment for her own needs. In fact, her rebellion against her own traditional role, which she sees as a rebellion against men, must also be a rebellion against her mother, who has sustained the concept of a man's world. The gifted girl, therefore, rejects her mother as an example. The young gifted girl, who is in enormous need of support and in need of a model, cannot find this in either her mother or her grandmother. In addition, because her mother's view of life has changed, that which used to be traditionally the domain of women, namely motherhood, becomes devaluated. The little girl feels this.

The second domain, which traditionally belongs to the child, namely childhood itself, has also been devaluated, for the mother may put it behind her own career in terms of priority. The gifted are even more conscious of this state of affairs. Just as the gifted girl used to feel inferior because she was a girl, she now feels inferior because she is a child. She knows that many people are deciding not to have children because they entail too much work. So while society is beginning to accept the rights of women and the rights of the gifted, it is devaluating and often ignoring the rights of children. What the gifted girl has gained on one side, she is losing on the other. Her mother is rebelling against her husband and putting her career first. She has less time for her little girl, who may have to witness her parents' separation, who may have to live in daily uncertainty as to her life's routine, and who, seeing a thousand little signs of not being valued, is left alone with the task of growing up. Growth without modeling is very difficult. There are as yet no definable models for women, let alone gifted women.

An unexpected phenomenon has developed. Giftedness as a characteristic has been redefined and is an accepted fact, but its goals and products are still basically defined only in terms of the male world. Women have to fight their way into this. They have to break into the men's world to fulfill themselves and often to support themselves. Therefore, at this point, the only definable model for the gifted girl is still the man. The woman becomes a doctor, not a nurse; she takes over the man's role and rejects that of the woman. The young gifted girl watches her mother trying to reach a goal which used to be restricted to men. The child, therefore, in order to fulfill her own needs and those expectations which society is now placing on her, must identify with her father. I recently observed this fact in many girls, and I was interested to find it supported by a recent newspaper article that reported on research that had been done about this question. It showed that modern young girls who are ambitious identify with their fathers.

What does this mean in terms of the psychosexual development of the young girl? Traditionally, the father is the young girl's love object and the person for whom she begins to develop her feminine characteristics, which means that she identifies with the mother in order to gain the father's love. How can the father now become both a love object and the person with whom the young girl identifies?

I believe that a new opportunity has opened for the young girl which allows her to actually outshine her mother in some respects. Although the father remains the child's love object, she realizes, of course, that actual physical seduction is taboo. Children have always learned to accept this fact as a reality. But now the ways are open to a new type of seduction: the intellectual one. The mother is still struggling with her traditional role while the little girl, who has not been raised in the same manner, does not feel held back from developing those gifts which used to belong only to boys. Therefore, instead of offering her femininity to her father, she offers her other gifts, or giftedness. She does not, in fact, need to feel guilty, for there is no taboo on intellectual intercourse. The father also can enjoy such a relationship without guilt or concern. Of course, this is not a completely new occurrence, but it is now becoming much more widespread. I have read in many autobiographies of famous women that they had a feeling of sharing a secret with their fathers. Fathers and daughters had something in common in which the mother, stuck in her stereotyped existence, could not participate. While the mother washed the dishes in the kitchen, the father and daughter enjoyed discussing the news.

This adds a new dimension to the basic relationship between men and women. I believe it can be defined as sublimated seduction, and will probably be carried over as an integral element in the girl's future relationships with men. It is in this way that modern gifted girls identify originally with their fathers, but then use this identification to try to win the father away from the mother.

I remember one particular case where this was very much out in the open. A brilliant little girl manipulated her parents to such an extent that she formed an intellectual alliance with her scientist father, one which her mother could not break. The father, in fact, shared a closer union with the daughter than he had with her mother. This led to enormous difficulties in the whole family structure.

I believe that this identification with the male is based on a well-known psychological process, namely the need to identify with those in power in order to gain power. At this point, signs of the next step in the development become visible. Women are beginning to define themselves in a new manner, which includes their newfound, expanded activities and emotions. We are beginning to look at a woman doctor as a phenomenon that is intrinsically different from a male doctor. This means that in the future the little girl will develop her own gifts by being able to identify with her own gifted mother. It also means that motherhood is included in the new definition of femininity. This, then, would also raise the status of childhood again.

Hopefully, we will find ways to make it possible for career and personality development not to contradict with motherhood and the responsibilities of raising children, but rather to become part of one integrated life. I know we are far from this in all practical aspects, but I feel that the need and possibilities are being recognized more and more.

Perhaps in a few years the gifted girl child will be surrounded by an ever-increasing number of feminine models in all areas of human society.

Looking back, I can see that we have gone through an exciting process of growth affecting women individually and as a group. Men have also grown because of this, and both sexes are beginning to meet again in a different and more satisfying manner. I am also hoping that this new trend in the definition of femininity and masculinity will have a beneficial effect on the manner in which we conduct the affairs of our world.

The Self-Image of the Gifted Child

Presented at a conference on gifted children at Oakland University, sponsored by the Academy for the Gifted and Talented, the Oakland Intermediate School District, Roeper City and Country School, and Oakland University, Oakland, Michigan (June, 1981).

If their infantile selves are surrounded by a protective cocoon of unconditional empathy, then they can face the world as a challenge, they can dare to enter it and experience trial-and-error; they can cope with whatever happens against a background of strength based on their parents' protection, and the mutual trust between them and their parents. However, if the protective cocoon does not exist, imagine the vulnerable, young underdeveloped self exposed to the impact of startling awareness beyond any emotional capacity to deal with it.

Self-image is one of the basic motivations for a person's actions, general behavior, growth, ability to learn, and ability to cope with life. Educators are beginning to recognize it as a major factor in the learning experience of all children and to see a good self-image as an educational goal (e.g., Canfield & Wells, 1976). In order to work with it, we need to define self-image, understand where it originates, and perceive how it grows and changes. Usually we connect it with the words "good" or "bad." We may say we need to help children develop a "good self-image."

What is self-image? What do we mean when we speak of a good or bad one? I believe that self-image is a complex concept embracing more than positive or negative feelings about oneself. It concerns a whole variety of judgments about one's self; in fact, I think they are endless. These judgments may include degrees of good and bad; they may also include practical assessments of one's abilities and accomplishments, weaknesses and strengths, and even our concept of the world and our role in it. It is our personal answer to such questions as: "Am I good-looking?" "Am I physically able?" "Am I a good student?" "Am I popular?"

But also: "Am I loved?" "Do my rights get consideration?" "What are my rights?" "Do I have any power over my destiny?" "Am I a worthwhile person?" "What is my role in the family, school, and society?" "Will I live up to my own expectations?" "Can I deal with this dangerous world?" "How am I dealing with my anger and hostilities, with my emotional needs, with my hopes and fears?" "Am I the only person to have bad thoughts, to have sexual fantasies...?" And, further, "Can I show myself as I really am, or do I have to present a mask or an as-if person to the outside world?"

Self-image consists of both conscious and unconscious feelings and opinions about oneself. A person could feel consciously that he or she is beautiful, bright and popular, and unconsciously that he or she is basically inferior and disappointing with no rights or power. It could also be the other way around. The "secret" self-image is therefore not only complex but maintains within itself contradictory notions. The strength of a person's ability to cope with life stems from his or her self-image.

Now the question is: How does the self-image develop? Related questions include: Where does it originate? Does it change along with developmental phases through which a person grows? Is there a biological factor involved? Is a child born with a certain self-image? There are many who would argue for the theory of biological determination. Recently I heard about the concept of the "resilient child." These children grow up under the most negative circumstances, yet cope with them well, while others who seem much better situated in life cannot cope. How is this to be explained? I believe that there might well be a biological component in terms of the extent of the child's inner strength to respond to his or her life experiences. If this factor is biologically determined, then it is out of our control. How the child's self-image develops, even given the biological basis, depends, however, on his or her environment and experiences. It is this area that we are concerned about.

I believe that much of the complex structure of self-image is based on very early experiences. A child is not born with images; they are implanted by encounters with the environment. The environment creates the basic framework within which the child's self-image grows and develops. It is defined by the reception the child receives at birth and the continuing series of expectations as he or she grows into adulthood. Do the parents consider the child their property, their own to fulfill their emotional needs, or do they recognize the child as an autonomous human being with the right for his or her own destiny, own emotions, own growth and accomplishments, failures and successes?

Do the parents love the child as their reflection and extension, or do they love the child as an independent person? If the former is the case, the child's self-image is based on how well he serves his parents' needs, for the child is completely dependent on his parents. He will not learn to love himself other than as a reflection of his parents' love. If the latter is the case, the child will learn to consider her own needs as legitimate. Erik Erikson (1963) speaks of the fact that the child's first task is to learn to trust the environment; out of this trust grows the basic framework for the self-image. It is the answer to the questions, "Can I trust my environment to develop myself?" "Do I own myself or am I owned by the environment?" As the child grows, the environment expands, and other people beyond the nuclear family make an impact on this basic framework. Once this framework is established, the child's self-image grows and changes according to individual characteristics and experiences. The way children see themselves develops out of what they expect of themselves and how they are able to live up to these expectations. This again is determined or influenced by the expectations of the environment and society.

What I have said so far is true for all people, gifted or not. The gifted, however, differ both in their expectations of themselves and also in their judgment of how they fulfill these expectations. They will therefore develop a different kind of self-image based on the different type of perception that they have of themselves and the world. I would like to share with you my experiences with gifted children and give you examples of how the self-images of some gifted children developed.

In my work with gifted children over the last 40 years, I have been aware of an ever-present phenomenon. The cognitive and creative development of these children are not in tune with their emotional reactions. Not only is there a dichotomy between their intellectual understanding and their emotional maturity, but the two factors seem to be in an unrealistic relationship to each other. In other words, the child's emotional reaction to his or her cognitive understanding or achievement often seems inappropriate. Also, the emotional reactions of the child to the reality of his or her situation in life frequently differ from what one would expect.

The subject itself has not yet been researched extensively, if at all. In order to find an answer to this question, which has struck me as mysterious over and over again, I have looked at Sigmund Freud's (1924/1952; 1925/1958) and Anna Freud's (1981) theories of child development, as well as Erik Erikson's (1963), Heinz Kohut's (1971) and Jean Piaget's (Piaget & Inhelder, 1964; Wolff, 1960) theoretical contributions. From all of these, I have developed a theory which at this point, at least in part, seems to illumine some of my observations. This is not the result of a carefully designed research project but is simply an attempt at explaining a phenomenon.

A child is born. Even during the first hours of life, there is a kind of taking in, a reaction, a desire to become acquainted with this new environment. Dim awareness slowly grows into primitive understanding. This process is faster and deeper with the gifted child. From the very beginning, there are present several strands of growth: cognitive, affective, and physical—in other words, thoughts, feelings, and bodily changes. They all influence each other in different ways as the child grows. Since these components develop differently within the gifted child, the influence they have on each other takes a different form in the gifted, and so does the end result.

Erik Erikson (1963) talks about the development of *trust* in the infant as the basis of its whole future development. Heinz Kohut (1971) speaks of the development of the self. How is the self nourished? How does it grow? It begins in the manner in which the child is received into this world. Will she have a right to a place of her own, or will she exist as an extension of her parents? Will she have a right to her own feelings, appropriate to each age and developmental stage? In other words, how do the parents feel about the child? For the child accepts the parents' expectations of her as her own, and she will face the world based on her parents' perception of her. It is this perception which allows the self to grow or to remain small and undeveloped.

Since the gifted have greater awareness than other children of the world and its complexities, they also have greater sensitivity to self based on their parents' expectations. This, then, makes the self of the gifted child even more vulnerable than that of others. Gifted children may understand interactions between their parents and comprehend their parents' reactions toward them (conscious and unconscious). At a very early age, they may notice inconsistencies. They may observe when siblings are treated differently; they may perceive dangers. If their infantile selves are surrounded by a protective cocoon of unconditional empathy, then they can face the world as a challenge, they can dare to enter it and experience trial-and-error; they can cope with whatever happens against a background of strength based on their parents' protection, and the mutual trust between them and their parents. However, if the protective cocoon does not exist, imagine the vulnerable, young underdeveloped self exposed to the impact of startling awareness beyond any emotional capacity to deal with it. This is the psychological dilemma of the gifted child.

Here are several examples of how these different parental approaches influence the self-development and self-images of gifted children.

EXAMPLE 1

A two-year-old child has a sudden attack of appendicitis and has to be rushed to the hospital to undergo an operation. Let's assume this happens to two children, both of them gifted, both able to talk and understand the process to some extent. One child is anxious and upset over the procedures and has a few nightmares following the operation. But he is interested in the process; he likes the explanation and likes to understand how his body functions. He understands that it had to be done in order to help him. This child overcomes his anxieties pretty soon because of his great trust in his parents and his realization that the surgery was done to help relieve his pain. His cognitive ability supported this understanding and made him able to master this traumatic experience.

Another child, also very bright, goes through a long period of sleep-lessness, is unable to venture out, and feels enormously anxious and very guilty. This child does not see herself as protected; she feels exposed to the newness of the hospital, the sudden operation and the pain, and feels that she has to deal with this all by herself without knowing what it is all about. Her giftedness only serves to make her more threatened because she is aware of what is happening to her but she does not feel supported by her parents. She also feels she must be a bad girl, that she is being punished for some reason. In the future, all of her successes serve only to let her parents know that she is really a good girl who deserves their support. However, she never believes that she is quite entitled to success because her parents would not have let her down had she not deserved it. This may, of course, happen to a child whether gifted or not. In the case of the gifted, it serves to explain the lack of gratification that an individual may get from personal success, while at the same time experiencing an enormous need to succeed over and over again. And, at times, her efforts may fail because she has the feeling that success is not her due. Failure, on the other hand, can be devastating to such a person. This individual, in childhood and adult life, views the world with feelings of powerlessness and lack of joy.

EXAMPLE 2

A father feels that he himself has been a failure; he realizes that his child is gifted. Soon the child becomes his second chance for success. The child realizes that his success now belongs to his father, feels that his father will take care of him as long as he succeeds, and that he exists solely for the purpose of giving his success to his father; without him, he is nothing. He has no right to his own feelings or achievements; in fact, his feelings have been relegated to the unconscious, for he is angry at his father for having deprived him of the ownership of his gift. However, all he is conscious of is his tremendous fear of failure. He has to succeed and be best or else all is lost, for his father, on whom he depends, will reject him if he does not provide success for him. And so he enjoys success because he has made his father happy.

But the depression, the desperation, can be overwhelming if he ever dares to fail. In his mind, his existence depends on succeeding—it is not a need for achievement, it is his very survival. All he knows is the pressure, the absolute obligation, to succeed. The origin of the pressure is unconscious because it comes from his earliest childhood. Also unconscious is the deep fury he has buried because his father has deprived him of the ownership of his success. This fury must be suppressed because he dares not express it toward his father. At some later time in his life, the process may become conscious, brought about by some experience or inner development, and an internal struggle ensues which then can be supported through therapy to allow him to own and enjoy his own gift for himself. If this does not happen, the child in him will continue to feel that he has to prove something to his father to earn his love, for he needs his father's love long after he has become an adult and the dependency ceases to be a reality.

If, however, the father views the child as an independent individual whom he needs to protect and nourish until he can stand on his own feet, then the child's success is his own and he can enjoy the father's pleasure in him as well as his independent success. In this case, he holds in his unconscious a feeling of support and belief in his abilities that he carries into his adult life.

Another possible consequence for a child who feels his parents have taken his gift away from him is becoming an underachiever. We have seen children where all efforts fail. The child will simply not achieve and use his gifts; no matter what kind of pressure or motivation is used, he remains an underachiever. Why is this? I believe it is his way of getting even with his father. He is very angry with his father for not letting him develop himself for himself. On the other hand, it would be too dangerous for him to allow himself feelings of anger against his father. Therefore, all he can feel is an inability to achieve or to concentrate or to make himself do those things that are necessary for him to do and that he is very capable of doing. All he and anyone else knows is that he is not living up to his potential. In reality, he is unconsciously withholding his gift from his father. He can do this only by denying the existence of his giftedness. In some sense, this child has more inner strength than the one described above, who feels he has to allow his father to own his gifts.

EXAMPLE 3

Some gifted children cannot see themselves as children. These are the children who cannot allow the teacher to teach them or a parent to tell them anything. They become troublemakers in school and cannot understand it when their superiority is challenged. The reason for this is not that these children want to show off. They want to shine because they distrust their parents to take care of them. They feel they must be in charge, not because they are great, but because they feel lack of support from their parents—lack of interest. "If I'm not great, everything goes to pieces." Their distrust of their parents is not conscious—they are only conscious of their desire to take charge, to have the power, for they cannot trust enough to allow somebody else to have power over them. This is a situation which happens with gifted children, for they are often truly able to be in charge. They have skills that are often far in advance of those of other children. They can figure out complex problems, and therefore in some ways feel they are adults and can take care of themselves. The psychological basis of their behavior, however, is that if they don't take care of themselves, no one will. Behind all of that superiority is an enormous anxiety that they will have to cope with something they are not really able to cope with. Such children need to be convinced that adults are to be trusted and that they can relax and be children.

EXAMPLE 4

It is well known that many gifted children are perfectionists. There are many reasons for this. Among them is the fact that realistically they often *are* the best; they often can do things better than everybody else. Perfectionism may also be due to circumstances described in the other examples, such as feeling that their success is owned by their parents. It is not, however, so well known that this perfectionism also extends to their feelings. Feelings also have to be perfect: Bad feelings are not allowed.

Other people may have negative feelings, but not this particular gifted child. He may not be aggressive, jealous, or afraid; these things are simply not an intelligent way of looking at life. This often becomes reinforced by parents who feel very strongly about being peaceful and settling disputes reasonably. Even though they may have every intention of supporting the child's feelings, he gets the message that anger and aggression are not acceptable.

Some children who are denied the expression of negative feelings tend to repress all feelings, good and bad. Good feelings as well as bad ones will be shoved into the unconscious. These are the people who have no noticeable affect. They may be telling a story which should have been very upsetting to them, and they smile when they tell it. These people have become separated from their feelings of self, and they feel as though they are nonexistent unless they are reflected in other people's responses. They see themselves only in others or in some physical reactions, such as pain, illness, drug-induced emotions, or even danger. These are the moments when these individuals know that they exist. I believe that feelings of nonexistence are more likely among the gifted, for they are the people for whom bad thoughts conflict with their drive toward personal perfection.

For this reason, it is particularly important that children realize early that even though parents believe in trying to be perfect and good, they are not always good; parents have feelings, too. It is necessary that parents express their feelings—even feelings of anger—as long as these feelings are grounded in a basic unconditional love of the child. In fact, the child will trust them more if they show themselves as they really are, as long as they remain intent on taking care of the child. Even though the child might be aware that his parents' power to protect him is limited, he will feel secure if they are authentic with him.

EXAMPLE 5

A young girl is gifted and successful. She relates well to her father because they have common interests. The child feels that her mother is jealous of her. In this case, the mother has not taken the gift away emotionally by making the child an extension of herself, but she resents the child's being gifted. In some cases, the mother is completely unaware of her own abilities. She begins to see her daughter as a rival. The girl has two reactions to this: On the one hand, she sees her mother's jealousy as a weakness, which tempts her to compete with her for her father's love. On the other hand, the mother then becomes a person who is on equal footing who cannot protect her, and the child becomes afraid and unrealistic in her expectations of herself. Her unconscious motivations, for she is not consciously aware of the jealousy and competition, are different from those of the children in the previous examples. I would say that she has more inner strength than the others because she does feel real support from her father. However, the normal family structure has been disrupted, and roles and responsibilities have been reversed.

EXAMPLE 6

A young child observes that her parents are having difficulties getting along with each other. She sees how they behave in an infantile manner in relating to each other, and their behavior to the child seems childish and unrealistic. She feels that no one in the family is supporting each other; they all seem unable to cope with life. However, because she is very gifted, she begins to feel that she understands things better than her parents, which actually may be the truth. She then sees no other way of surviving herself but to see herself as the leader of the family—as the only one who can be protective. These children carry an enormous burden of imagined responsibility way beyond their years. I have seen children who seemed to carry the weight of the world on their shoulders, and they may even express it in words. They may be aware of their own inability to carry this load and the inappropriateness of their feelings of omnipotence; yet, unconsciously, they have to take charge, for they feel there is no one else. The reason for this is again unconscious. It is true distrust of their parents' ability to cope. In the case described above, the girl doesn't distrust her parents' love for her, but rather their ability to take care of her. She is likely to become a caretaker throughout her life, more aware of other people's needs than her own.

These are only a few of the examples of the world of the unconscious in the development of the young gifted child. Space does not permit me to delve more deeply into this topic. The purpose of this paper has been to begin to take a look at the role of the unconscious of the gifted in the development of their self-images. It is my hope that I may have created an understanding of the care with which we need to treat the development of the self of the gifted child. Hopefully, by making this need conscious we will help more gifted people develop truly integrated personalities. It is my further hope that my thoughts might stimulate further research into this subject.

References

Canfield, J., & Wells, H.C. *100 Ways to Enhance Self-Concept in the Classroom: A Handbook for Teachers and Parents.* Englewood Cliffs, NJ: Prentice-Hall, 1976.

Erikson, E.H. *Childhood and Society.* New York: W. W. Norton and Company, 1963. (Original work published in 1950.)

Freud, A. *The Writings of Anna Freud: Volume 8. Psychoanalytic Psychology of Normal Development.* New York: International Universities Press, 1981.

Freud, S. *A General Introduction to Psychoanalysis* (J. Riviere, Trans.). New York: Washington Square Press, 1952. (Original work published in 1924.)

—*On Creativity and the Unconscious* (J. Riviere, Trans.). New York: Harper & Row, 1958. (Original work published in 1925.)

Kohut, H. *The Analysis of the Self.* New York: International Universities Press, 1971.

Piaget, J., & Inhelder, B. *The Early Growth of Logic in the Child.* New York: Harper & Row, 1964.

Wolff, P.H. *The Developmental Psychologies of Jean Piaget and Psychoanalysis.* New York: International Universities Press, 1960.

How Gifted Children Cope
with Their Emotions

Presented at the Fourth World Conference of the World Council for the Gifted in Montreal, Quebec, Canada (August, 1981). Subsequently printed in *The Roeper Review,* vol. 5, no. 2 (November, 1982).

Emotions cannot be treated separately from intellectual awareness or physical development. All three intertwine and influence each other.

During my years as headmistress and co-founder of the Roeper City and Country School, I became aware of gifted children's emotions, motivations, abilities, frustrations, and anxieties from a developmental point of view. The following thoughts, which are illumined by my background in psychoanalytic and educational theory, are based not on formal research but on my direct observation of gifted children. I wish to focus on how their uniquely formed characteristics interrelate to form the total personality of gifted children.

Interest in gifted children is focused primarily on their intellectual and creative characteristics rather than on their emotional nature. There is, however, an awareness of the dichotomy between their intellectual and emotional development, the intellectual viewed as advanced and the emotional as normal or slow. I believe this model to be inaccurate and detrimental in planning for the gifted child. A child is a total entity, a combination of many characteristics. Emotions cannot be treated separately from intellectual awareness or physical development. All three intertwine and influence each other. A gifted five-year-old does not function or think like an average ten-year-old. He does not feel like an average ten-year-old, nor does he feel like an average four- or five-year-old. Gifted children's thoughts and emotions differ from those of other children, and as a result they perceive and react to their world differently.

For example, a gifted three-year-old may understand what injury means, but not having the experience of a six-year-old, he may not know the difference between a bad injury and a less dangerous one. In acting out normal feelings of jealousy, he may hit his baby brother with a block, and at the same time believe that he is not supposed to be jealous. He feels this more strongly than an average three-year-old would feel. He is also aware that hitting his brother might result in injury. Therefore, this child feels much greater guilt than another child his age would feel about the same kind of behavior.

Although gifted children's emotions and intellects are different, they are not necessarily more advanced. These characteristics can only be understood if they are examined as a unit, for giftedness cannot be defined in separate categories such as intellectual giftedness, creative giftedness, or physical giftedness. These categories always act upon one other, although some may be more apparent in some individuals than others. In short, giftedness entails a greater degree of awareness and sensitivity and a greater ability to understand and transform perceptions into intellectual and emotional experiences.

There is a difference between giftedness and precociousness. Precocious children grasp certain concepts sooner than other children, while gifted children understand their depth and complexity. The gifted think and feel in global terms, experience connections, and see the whole rather than the parts. They conceptualize in more sophisticated categories. This is not a purely intellectual activity, but an emotional experience. A young gifted child, for instance, may feel that a spoon, a fork, and a knife belong together in a single category because one needs all three to eat a meal. A precocious child, on the other hand, may put things into normal categories more quickly, such as grouping knives with knives.

An example: Two gifted seven-year-olds developed a close relationship based on their interest in playing chess. One child was Jewish, the other Arabic. Their parents took strongly opposing views during the Six Day War between Israel and the Arab countries, and these children were confronted with a most painful conflict. They became interested in the war, learned much about it, upheld political positions similar to those of their parents, yet still remained good friends. The children had a deep commitment to these conflicting perceptions. They saw themselves as Jew and Arab, respectively, yet still viewed each other as friends. The conflict was unresolvable for them.

If these children had been less gifted, they might not have become so involved in the conflict or drawn any consequences from it for their own relationship. Or they might have seen each other as enemies and separated over this issue. As gifted children, they were able to see each other's viewpoint and, as a result, were unable to find a simple solution because they were very aware of the complexities of the conflict. Had these children been average 16-year-olds, they would have seen the problem, become deeply involved in the issues, and probably would have severed their personal relationship. Had they been gifted 16-year-olds, they probably would have dealt with the problem together and arrived at a solution independent of their parents.

Gifted children go through the same developmental stages as other children, but in a different manner. As a result, they develop different types of self-images. I am aware, of course, that these types are generalizations and that no one particular child may be completely described by any one category. However, these types do describe some common approaches gifted children choose to cope with their emotions.

The Perfectionist

Many gifted children become perfectionists and remain so as adults. They do not give themselves permission to fail in anything they undertake, particularly in whatever they define as their specific field of competency. To fail is a right for others, but not for themselves; their emotional need is to be perfect. This, of course, is an unrealistic demand.

It is normal for young children to feel omnipotent, but many gifted children carry this feeling of omnipotence beyond the normal stage. While other children discover the limits of their power and ability by trial-and-error, gifted children are often able to fulfill their wishes without severe limitations. These children are admired for being special, and their parents are often in awe of them. The children misinterpret their parents' behavior while constantly reinforcing it by manipulating the environment more successfully than average children. It therefore becomes the mandate of these children to accomplish anything they want to do. If, however, they find that they are unable to live up to these expectations, they consider it their personal fault rather than a realistic limitation of their age and ability. They often feel pressured and guilty whenever failure occurs, which leads to feeling inferior, for there are many such occasions when they cannot meet their own goals.

Another phenomenon related to the feeling of omnipotence is that the superego of gifted children may develop at an unusually early age because of their sensitivity and awareness. In these cases, the continuation of omnipotence coincides with an early development of conscience, and together they create an unusual alliance. In the more average child, the feeling of omnipotence is limited by reality before the conscience develops. In combination, however, the feeling of omnipotence and the development of conscience turn into an enormous obligation. Feelings of omnipotence make children believe that there is no limit to their abilities, while the newly developed conscience forces them to act with moral perfection. In other words, they feel that their ability to achieve has no limitation and it is their duty to live up to this unlimited capacity. Imagine the burdens these children take upon themselves, feeling responsible for everything and feeling guilty every time they fail to live up to their responsibility.

The environment often serves to support this illusion, for teachers and parents tend to take advantage of children's giftedness. A father who perceives himself as unsuccessful sees a second chance for himself in his gifted son, and conveys to his son the feeling that he must succeed in all he does in order to fulfill the father's needs. The child feels that his father loves and supports him only for his gifts; yet he, too, clearly needs unconditional support, just as every child does. The child's fear of failure is tremendous, for he cannot afford to fail and disappoint his father, nor can he enjoy his successes because he does not own them. His only reward is his father's pleasure.

Another illustration is a nine-year-old girl who enters a school for gifted children. She received all A's in her previous school, and her family was very proud of her. In the new school, no grades are given; instead, the school uses the open classroom approach, in which students work at their own level and on their own interests. The girl cannot be the best or earn honors or awards in the new school, for none are given. She cannot endure this structure and philosophy and becomes depressed because her measure for self-esteem, namely the gift to her parents of her success over others, has been taken away from her.

Another frequent consequence of the combination of omnipotence and conscience extends to the emotions. For instance, gifted children often believe that negative emotions are not possible for themselves. Other people are allowed to be angry, aggressive, jealous, or afraid, but not they, since these kinds of feelings are deemed imperfect and must therefore be eliminated. Because these feelings cannot be eliminated, they are generally suppressed and relegated to the unconscious. As a result, certain symptoms and feelings remain, such as guilt, fear, worries, and phobias.

At times, the denial of negative feelings leads to a complete separation of the affective domain, particularly when positive as well as negative feelings are suppressed and a lack of affect and feeling becomes evident in the child's behavior. On occasion, these children develop a feeling of depersonalization, a feeling of not truly existing. For example, a young girl felt that an event only took place when she shared it with someone else. She wrote to her absent friend every day, for only then did she feel her experiences had really happened. She needed others to verify her existence.

When these children do express their emotions, the results are generally underdeveloped and explosive because of inexperience. For example, a very gifted boy still had many fears that he had acquired as a small child. Adjusting to a new teacher, starting a new project, and moving to a new house were all difficult experiences for him, and he reacted to them with anxiety and uncertainty. His self-expectations were extremely high, and he required much adult support. He never fought, however, for he thought fighting was silly. As a young adolescent, he hit another child and was overcome with guilt. One could say that his true feelings were expressed at this moment, in spite of his intentions not to allow this to happen—that is, to act aggressively and in opposition to his own self-image. He was overcome with terror and cried and could not be consoled for a long time. This kind of behavior was not perfect, and it was perfection that he expected of himself.

In other cases, suppressed aggression is expressed against the person's own self. These people may become masochists, placing themselves in situations in which they become scapegoats. In extreme cases, this kind of suppressed aggression, finally expressed, can lead to suicide. I have heard a number of gifted children say that they wished to be like computers, for computers have no emotions to interfere with perfect thought.

The Child/Adult

Some gifted children see themselves as adults and feel in complete charge of themselves. Anything that interferes with this vision is a threat to their self-image. They observe the weaknesses of adults and feel that they can trust only themselves.

These children are often identified as underachievers. They do not allow themselves to be learners because they cannot accept the position of being a peer to other children. They do not accept adult authority and often have behavior problems, not because of any aggressive behavior, but because they need to maintain the illusion of being in charge. The demands of teachers and parents seem to interfere with what they consider their rightful position. They do not understand why they cannot refrain from reacting strongly to being considered a child.

The need to be in charge is unconscious. These children cannot afford emotionally to give up power, so they do all they can to maintain a position that is unrealistic and vulnerable. They view the world as a threat; their need to be in charge is a struggle for survival, one they defend with all their power. For them, it takes too much trust to be a child.

These children also react to the insecurities and weaknesses of their parents, who often promote the idea that their children are, in fact, superior. The children feel unprotected and on their own while confronted with an unknown world. Thus, the child/adult has two antagonists: the dangers and unknown problems of the world, which they cannot really master, and the continued threat to their unrealistic positions and self-image by their environment, which treats them as the children they are. This may cause paranoia, for they come to believe that no one is trustworthy but themselves.

Other children react differently. They may not as readily perceive parental weaknesses, nor do they believe unrealistically in their own superior strength and ability. They understand that there is no choice other than to accept the position of being dependent children. Therefore, they may not battle with their surroundings. Confronted with the limits of their own abilities, they know that it is impossible to be an adult.

Child/adults are in many ways like perfectionists, but with one important difference. Perfectionists have a tendency to diminish their feelings of self-worth and their rights to their own emotions; they may donate their gift to their parents and subordinate their own emotional needs. Child/adults, on the other hand, defend their infantile selves against the world and feel that they are the only ones capable of doing so.

The Winner of the Competition

Gifted children go through the same psychosexual developmental phases as do other children, but often in a different manner. An example is the four-year-old boy who loves his mother and wants to take his father's place. Most children go through this period of competition, but they realize that Father is there to stay and has abilities that they have not yet acquired. The gifted child, however, may feel that he is truly the winner of the competition, particularly when his parents are in awe of him.

The child feels smarter and more capable than his father and sees himself as the mother's partner, which makes him feel like an adult. Consequently, he is forced to frantically maintain this position and compete constantly with his father. He carries this competitiveness everywhere, believing that he must do better than all of his peers to show his mother how great he is. His need for support from his father is relegated to the unconscious. Still, he harbors many fearful questions: Can I really remain in this position? Will my father take revenge on me?

Unconsciously, the child does not really want to be victorious over his father; he would, in fact, prefer to be cared for by his father and simply be a child. Yet the temptation to be victorious is great. The father may support the competition because he is jealous of the child and feels that his son has taken the mother's affection away from him.

The roles again are reversed, and as such, the winner of the competition is similar in many ways to the child/adult. However, the winner of the competition generally has a well-established, realistic concept of himself and may feel parental support. Nevertheless, he experiences an even greater conflict than others in passing through the Oedipal period, and the resolution of the conflict may be delayed into a stage where it is inappropriate and no longer expected. Where the child/adult fights for his basic security, the winner of the competition fights for an imagined right.

The Exception

There are gifted children whose feelings of omnipotence interfere with their development of conscience. Most children learn early on that their wishes cannot always be fulfilled because they may conflict with the needs of others. This experience forces them to realize that others have legitimate needs and rights that may or may not correspond to their own needs. Through this process, children learn to identify with others and develop empathy.

For some gifted children, however, their abilities lead to great personal power that is never reconciled with the needs of others. As a result, these children do not develop feelings for others, and they tend to use their abilities to fulfill only their own wishes and needs. Their giftedness leads to an impairment of the normal development of identification, empathy, and conscience. They remain fixated in a period of infantile self-centeredness. Such gifted children live on very shaky ground. Because it is this difference upon which they base their self-esteem, they must maintain the illusion of being outside the rules and regulations that govern the lives of normal people. If they had to see themselves realistically, to give up this image, they would lose the foundation for their self-esteem.

Parents often unconsciously support this self-centeredness by believing that their children are so special that they do not need to live within normal social limitations. For example, a mother of a highly gifted high school student felt that it was demeaning for her child to follow the rule that all students, regardless of age, must be seated on the school bus. She felt it might interfere with her son's creativity. The boy developed into a very clever delinquent who had no understanding of the rights of others.

The exceptions among gifted children are like the perfectionists because both unrealistically perceive their abilities. The exceptions are unlike the perfectionists, however, in that they underestimate their responsibilities. The exceptions are like child/adults because they feel superior to adults but, unlike child/adults, they see themselves as beyond the system. The exceptions are also similar to the winners of the competition in that both feel superior to the parent of the opposite sex. However, the exceptions feel that competition is not required, for normal expectations do not apply to them. Their journey through the developmental phases is altered by their fixation on the feeling of omnipotence.

The Self-Critic

Some gifted children tend to view themselves critically and find themselves wanting. Their emotions, actions, thoughts, and behaviors do not live up to their expectations. It is as though they can separate from themselves and evaluate themselves objectively.

The self-critics spend their time and energy criticizing themselves and their work. They feel compelled to do a task over and over again. They are overwhelmed with all their obligations because everything has to be checked and rechecked. Their behavior becomes compulsive. They often fail at tasks because they have so much difficulty carrying out their intentions. Such children feel that it is their obligation to reform the world around them; at the same time, they see themselves as incapable of doing so. They have given up their feeling of omnipotence early but have overextended their conscience. Yet their insights, deep awarenesses, and even self-criticism originate from their giftedness. This type differs from all the types previously described because they do not believe in their giftedness, only in their responsibilities.

The Well-Integrated Child

There are many gifted children who pass through the developmental phases in a normal manner. They are the children who feel supported by their parents in a manner that allows them to see themselves as autonomous human beings who own their giftedness. They view themselves realistically, understand that failure is a part of learning, and realize that positive and negative emotions are basic components of life. They overcome their feelings of omnipotence in a normal manner and develop a more realistic conscience at the proper developmental phase. However, these children are also aware that they are different from other children as a consequence of their giftedness.

Well-integrated children are often more aware of the world's problems and feel compelled to stand up for their convictions, but suffer loneliness and isolation for taking such risks. At such times, they need the continued support of the family, not so much for their actions but for the resulting feelings created by their reactions to their surroundings. When these feelings are recognized by the children and their families as appropriate, the children's emotional needs are supported and they can use their gifts to cope with their negative feelings according to the normal phase through which they are passing.

Such children are free to develop constructive activities and to grow emotionally, as well as cognitively and creatively. They realize that they have a legitimate right to their own feelings as well as to their gifts. On that basis, they develop empathy for the feelings of others. Their energies are free to develop their abilities, for they recognize their positive as well as negative feelings as both normal and human. This does not mean that they will not encounter difficulties, failures, and problems, but only that they are better equipped to cope with them. These children can enjoy their gifts.

Although giftedness is often defined by one aspect of the individual which is most apparent, I am reluctant to separate that one aspect for fear of not considering the total person. Nevertheless, it is helpful to be aware of the particular aspect of giftedness in the person that is most apparent if we are to understand the needs of gifted children. For example, a child can be driven by interests in math to the exclusion of other learning.

My observations raise the following questions: Can a person be emotionally gifted? Can a person have a particular emotional strength that makes this aspect of their personality the most outstanding one? Does the ability to integrate the emotions with the intellect, creativity, and physical growth depend on the response of adults, or is this also an innate capacity of the child?

I believe there are people who have such gifts. They have the capacity to integrate their emotions, intellect, and creativity against enormous odds. They deal realistically with life and move normally through their developmental phases. I have observed children who are particularly sensitive to their own and to other people's feelings and who dare to act upon this awareness.

Some gifted children show enormous empathy for others, surpassing at times the compassion of adults who are more limited by society's expectations. As a result, adults may not understand gifted children's reactions. For example, during a chess tournament, John, who is clearly in the lead, begins to make careless mistakes and loses the match. When asked what happened, he replies, "I noticed my opponent had tears in his eyes. I couldn't concentrate, and I lost my desire to win." John's empathy was greater than his ambition. Many adults, especially those who support John, will be disappointed. Yet one could argue that his reaction is a more mature one than theirs, for his self-esteem does not depend on winning the competition.

Summary

The perfectionist is one who combines the early phase of omnipotence with the later phase of superego or conscience development. I have seen this constellation influence the developmental growth of children between the ages of three and twelve. The child/adult is one who combines the feeling of omnipotence with an unrealistic concept of total independence. I have seen this attitude present in very young children. The winner of the competition is one who combines the feeling of omnipotence and the Oedipal phase, often extending the Oedipal stage beyond normal age limits. I have seen children struggling with this at ages ten, eleven, and twelve. In the case of the exception, the feeling of omnipotence remains an overpowering force that keeps normal growth from occurring. Even as an adult, this person remains infantile. The self-critic, by contrast, overcomes the feeling of omnipotence early and remains fixated on strong superego development.

All of these types of gifted children suffer in their self-development because the developmental phases have been met unevenly. Their giftedness has altered the manner in which they go through the normal developmental phases. This, in turn, makes an impact on their personality and self-image. Well-integrated gifted children, on the other hand, proceed through developmental phases in a normal manner and meet the experiences they encounter against a background of emotional strength and balance.

It is my belief that concern for the emotional development of the gifted should become part of the educational process. I am hoping that more research will be done in this area, and that parents, social workers, psychologists, administrators, and teachers will become interested in this aspect of gifted children.

References

Freud, A. *Normality and Pathology in Childhood: Assessment and Development.* London: International Universities Press, 1965.

Greenacre, P. *Emotional Growth: Psychoanalytic Studies,* Vol. II. New York: International Universities Press, 1971.

Hesse, H. *Beneath the Wheel.* New York: Bantam Books, 1968.

Kohlberg, I. *Collective Papers on Moral Development and Moral Education.* Blue Book. Cambridge: Moral Education and Research Foundation, 1973.

—*Collective Papers on Moral Development and Moral Education.* Yellow Book, Cambridge: Moral Education and Research Foundation, 1975.

Kohut, H. *The Analysis of the Self.* New York: International Universities Press, 1971.

Maier, H. *Three Theories of Child Development.* New York: Harper & Row, 1965.

Miller, A. *Prisoners of Childhood.* New York: Basic Books, Inc., 1981.

Roeper, A. "Some Observations about Gifted Pre-School Children." *Journal of Nursery Education,* 9 (3), (1963).

—"Normal Phases of Emotional Development and the Young Gifted Child." Roeper Publications, 12 (4), (1977).

Stress Can Be a Positive Force
in Gifted Children

Lecture given at the University of New Brunswick, New Brunswick, Canada (1984).

Some gifted children seem much more resilient to stress than others. Some even seem to invite it. We may not be able to fully understand gifted children's differences in response to stress, but we must provide them with the resources to deal with it.

Gifted children experience pressure and stress from two main sources: the environment and themselves. Some of the outside pressures are common to all gifted people. We live in a world geared to the average, where most thought processes and resulting actions are simple. They are often based on single classifications and single contrasts. Gifted children, however, see and react to the complexity of the problems surrounding them and act accordingly. They see the gray areas, the overlaps, and the contradictions. Consequently, gifted children are out of step with their environment, and this ever-present difference is a stress-producing element for a number of reasons.

Before we can appreciate the ways in which gifted children are subject to stress, we need to explore what this term means. What is stress? In the most elemental sense of the word, it means pressure, impact. In order for stress to exist, there must be something that receives it, something on which something else makes an impact. Stress exists only if there is something to be stressed.

We say that an individual "receives" stress. But *how* does this happen? And *what* in the person receives the stress? The heart? The left brain or right brain? In my opinion, how a person reacts to all experiences, including stress, depends on the state, the development, and the uniqueness of the person, the most inner self of the person. It is the self that experiences stress. The self is the beholder, and stress is in the eye of the beholder.

And so we are forced to consider another question: What is the self? The self, I believe, is the interior of a person to which everything else is exterior. Stress usually develops out of the relationship between the inner and outer selves; sometimes it stems from only the inner self. Are the inner and outer selves in tune with one another? Are they partners, or are they antagonists? This relationship depends on the shape of each— the self and the world. Education at its best can be defined as the positive nurturing of this relationship. In itself, stress is neither negative nor positive. It depends, rather, on how the self receives it and on the state of the self. I believe that stress can be a positive force under the right conditions. Just how it can be so, I will explore later in this talk. But first I want to turn my attention to the ways in which stress affects gifted children.

Because of their complex thought processes, gifted children are misunderstood or not understood at all. They get negative feedback, or they experience a certain perplexed reaction, or they get no feedback at all. They are not likely to receive appropriate feedback. Other children, less complex in their thoughts, get the exchange of ideas and reactions they expect to receive. There is little or no exchange of ideas on the level of gifted children, and that creates unfulfilled needs and stress. These children are likely to work alone on their projects and thoughts. They have a lack of intellectual or creative interchange. Because they get no resonance for their ideas, they become bored, and boredom is very stressful because it means being unfulfilled. If, however, their giftedness is understood because they produce an identifiable product, such as learning how to read at an early age or achieving outstanding success in math, a different type of stress occurs: being exploited by one's parents and teachers. In this case, it is the gift that gets the attention, not the person. This, too, creates a certain kind of stress. For example, children who already know how to read in kindergarten will most likely be called upon to read when visitors are present. Even though they enjoy the attention they receive, they realize that it is their gift, not themselves as persons, that receives the attention.

Other pressures that gifted children experience are produced by the fact of the giftedness itself. These pressures include:

- Recognizing the state of the world and the dangers that surround us and being unable to do anything about it.

- Realizing that adults are also unable, and often are unwilling, to face the global situation. For example, many young gifted children react with enormously complex feelings to the fact that we are living in a nuclear age. They are fearful and feel powerless in the face of this, and consequently are angry at complacent, short-sighted adults. At the same time, they have an intellectual interest in the fact of the nuclear development itself. They are also apt to wonder about their own futures and what kinds of plans to make in view of the danger of nuclear annihilation.

- Recognizing injustices in personal life as well as society. These create a number of stresses and strong feelings, such as anger, frustration, and a compulsion to do something useful. But gifted children feel powerless to make an impact. They are lonely because no one else seems to care about the obvious injustice of the situation. Average children, especially the young, are not concerned with problems or injustices that happen in faraway places or even in their own environment. Gifted children, by contrast, often make these problems their own.

The personal pressures do not always relate to the here and now or to actual events, but to worries and concerns about the future. The future is real to gifted children, and they react to it at an early age. They also are concerned at an early age with death, but they do not know how to handle it either emotionally or intellectually. They know that they cannot escape it. They are concerned with hostility and aggression and recognize it more strongly than others do. They do not know how to handle this either. They are afraid of failure and hate to experience it.

One of the greatest pressures on gifted children is the pressure to be perfect. Because of this, they often have unrealistic expectations and standards for themselves and strive desperately to achieve them. On the other hand, they also fear their own superiority in competitive situations because they do not want to receive negative reactions from others, especially when, as is often the case, these others include their own parents. They also may suffer from the opposite pressure, namely, the urgent need to win competitions. Their need for perfection shows clearly their lack of personal power because they are not able to be perfect. They realize that they are small selves surrounded by a large awareness. They deeply perceive their helplessness.

In addition, gifted children experience stress from the complexities they realize. They cannot categorize things as easily as other children. They cannot pursue goals as completely because they always see the other side of the argument and the consequences of certain actions. This leads to great difficulty in making commitments and often leaves them outside of groups. Normal children, who think in simple terms, can accept goals more easily as their own, whereas to gifted children everything may seem relative. They find it difficult to make an absolute commitment to a single position. On the other hand, they feel the pressure to be deeply involved and to reach for certain goals, but they encounter impediments that prevent their attaining them in daily life. This creates stress and results in irritation.

Additional stress is produced because the stress on the gifted may not be recognized by others, or may be misunderstood, or may not be viewed as legitimate by teachers and parents. Such children, therefore, do not receive recognition, relief, or help. Stress needs to be relieved by whatever means possible, but at times this is not possible because the stress suffered by gifted children may not be recognized. The stress they experience is not ordinary stress. For example, a gifted child may not be heartbroken if she loses a spelling bee, but her inability to express her complicated, deep thoughts in an English composition may send her into a depression, even if the teacher is perfectly satisfied with the quality of her work.

Another example: A high school boy is in trouble because he does not do his homework, although he really would like to. In addition, he is desperate because he is not given time to finish the symphony he has on his mind all the time. He is under two types of stress: outer stress to do his homework and to fulfill normal expectations, and inner stress prompted by his own creativity. Probably neither of these is recognized by adults, for they see no reason for him not to do his homework. They do not understand how it feels to be pressured to finish an incomplete symphony that one hears in one's head.

Gifted children need feedback even more than adults do. Often their goals and achievements do not receive any kind of recognition, while conventional goals which are common to everyone are applauded. This leaves gifted children all alone with their goals and achievements. Out of this grows yet another source of stress. There seems to be a basic need in every human being to measure one's achievements or abilities against a norm. Gifted children, however, often have goals and achievements for which there is no means of measurement, so they may not be recognized by others at all. How, then, do gifted children know that they are achieving whatever goals they have set for themselves? Albert Einstein and Albert Schweitzer, for instance, had types of giftedness that bore tangible results. They received positive feedback, but this happened only late in their lives. Many other gifted people never receive positive feedback for their goals and accomplishments precisely because they cannot be measured. How do we measure understanding that is more complex than that of others? And how can gifted children maintain their drive in the face of indifference or scorn?

Another source of stress for gifted children is the lack of role models. Because they often move in new directions, there are no models for them to follow. It is like the explorer who thinks she will make a discovery, but since it has not been made before, she cannot be sure. Many gifted people have original thoughts and ideas and create original products that may not be accepted. It is no accident that gifted people seldom become rich from their work and have to pursue other occupations in order to be able to carry out their real desires. They seldom receive medals or applause, and if they do, it is more likely to happen much later in life. Therefore, many people lose motivation and interest, and their giftedness never flourishes. It is hard to be one of a kind. All of this, of course, often creates a social type of pressure because gifted children have a tendency to be loners. But they also need the company and support of peers and adults.

There is another dimension of how stress affects gifted children. They not only receive stress, but also create it. Gifted children create a kind of discomfort in their surroundings, for by their mere existence they uncover hidden shortcomings. Their expectations are unconventional, and society finds itself unable to fulfill them. The gifted high school student who would rather write a symphony than do homework has been led to believe that his education will fulfill his personal needs. He finds out, however, that this is not the case. His disappointment in the environment's failure to fulfill its promise creates a sense of disappointment in his surroundings.

The gifted do not accept neat, simple categories; they expect society to think in complex terms, as they do. They expect society to look honestly at itself and to perceive things about itself which it cannot and does not want to see. It is always a source of amazement to see how well gifted children know their teachers and parents. The children are aware of both the strengths and the weaknesses of the adults. They expect the adults' behavior to be consistent with their words. They do not understand when adults say, "Do as I say, not as I do."

At the same time, gifted children feel that they are expected to look up to adults. They sense when adults feel threatened and insecure, even when they pretend otherwise. In that case, children feel betrayed in their sense of justice. And because they cannot accept this, they challenge adults' authority and superiority. For example, an adult may feel free to drink alcohol, a known drug, and yet condemn his child for taking drugs. These types of things become an enormous puzzle for all children, but the gifted are less ready to accept them and will voice their opinions. This threatens society's accepted order, and is therefore experienced as a threat.

Average people are superior to the gifted only in terms of their numbers. Such people counteract the threat of the gifted by isolating them. The gifted are frequently considered strange. They might talk too much, they might be too insistent, they might be do-gooders, they might always be reading, etc. They make others feel uneducated. Intellectualism does not have positive connotations in our society, which often reacts negatively to its gifted people as a way to counteract the stress they create. It has often been observed that the gifted have a tendency toward suicide. It is equally true that society has a tendency to render the gifted ineffectual in whatever way possible. It wants to escape the challenge and stress produced by them.

If we look at history, we might say that average people are exposed to the danger of murder, but gifted people are exposed to the danger of assassination. Examples include Caesar Augustus, Dr. Martin Luther King, Jr., Abraham Lincoln, John Fitzgerald Kennedy, and many, many others. Aristotle was thrown into prison. Jesus Christ was crucified. It has often been observed that we treat older people with a lack of respect. Could it be that we fear that they have accumulated some kind of wisdom that we do not want to hear? The same might be true for the gifted.

The stress created by gifted children naturally comes back as more stress to them. How do gifted children cope with these various types of stress? Each individual experiences stress in a different manner and each develops his or her own coping mechanisms. What goes unnoticed by one may become a major problem for another. The reasons for this are often incomprehensible to the casual observer. Some gifted children seem more resilient to stress than others; some even seem to invite stress. We may not be able to fully understand gifted children's differences in response to stress, but we must provide them with the resources to deal with it.

I said earlier that stress can be a positive force under the right conditions. How? The first and most important way in which we can help gifted children is to give them the strength to cope with stress. We can do that by recognizing that the growth of the self is a part of the educational process. We have a tendency to feel that, for gifted children, emphasis must be placed on their intellectual development only. I believe that the development of intellectual potential depends on the development of the self. In fact, we cannot separate one from the other. It is this very separation that makes gifted children feel stress as a negative force. The foundation for the development of the self is laid in very early childhood. It begins with the way parents feel about their children. Young children feel about themselves the way their parents feel about them. They have no other source of judgment. Their feelings mirror those of their parents. Do parents view their children as extensions of themselves to fulfill their own needs? When this is so, children's selves depend on their parents, and they cannot develop a sense of autonomy. There is a lack, an unfulfilled need. We must, therefore, look at ourselves, our own needs, and see how we tend to relate them to children.

This is true in a different way for the teacher also. We need to see children as separate, autonomous beings. Birth is separation.

The next way in which we can help gifted children to cope with stress is to have empathy for them. The goal is not to identify with them, but to empathize with who they are and to try to fulfill their needs as much as we can. Of course, we need to balance this with the reality of the family situation, the needs of other children, and our own needs, but we need to look at gifted children on their own terms, not measure them against Johnny and Suzy next door. This is not the same as being permissive. It does not mean that we have to follow children's wishes and desires all the time, because these may not be what they really need. It simply means thinking in terms of children rather than in terms of the arbitrary expectations of the world. As they grow older, the form that empathy for children takes changes. Stress then relates to the kinds of pressures that the gifted child is exposed to. It may relate, for instance, to the perfectionism or to the specific learning process that is typical for an individual child. Awareness of what the pressures are will help us to have the necessary empathy with gifted children.

It is important that young children feel protected by us against both inner and outer pressures. I believe that children need to see this protection as a kind of cocoon that allows them to develop their selves so that they will be increasingly able to protect themselves and to deal with the pressures, desires, and excitement of growing up.

One of the pressures gifted children face is being confronted with the confusion and the chaos of the world. They have an enormous desire to make sense of it all, to understand the structure of the world. This is the basis for their motivation to learn. We have a tendency to try and steer them into our conventional processes and educational goals. These result in outer success, while what they really need in order for their selves to grow and to turn pressures into positive forces is to master the world, to incorporate a system and a structure, and to make it their own rather than see it as alien and threatening.

We must recognize the different phases the self goes through in the process of growth and cope with them in an appropriate manner. Gifted children grow somewhat differently from other children. It is helpful if parents are aware of these phases and develop a willingness and ability to help their children whenever they are confronted with new stresses due to different developmental phases.

Gifted children have a great desire to learn, grow, and express themselves. We can help them by enjoying this growth with them and participating in it as people who also want to learn and grow. It is amazing how much we can learn from them if we are willing to keep our eyes open and look where they are looking. New discoveries are made by even the youngest gifted child many times during the day.

Gifted children who have a strong and independent sense of self will turn pressures into positive forces. Due to their greater awareness, they will see real dangers at an earlier age than other children and develop an appropriate sense of fear in response to them. Gifted children who feel good about themselves will be more careful to protect themselves and others. They can, for instance, be trusted at a much earlier age not to walk into traffic or expose themselves to other physical dangers. In fact, they will not tackle a task until they have mastered the inner or outer skill it requires. For example, they will not jump into a body of water unless they can swim. They are not as likely to take drugs during adolescence. They will drive a car carefully and not fool around with it while they are driving. They will maintain a healthy sense of fear. They will, in fact, try to pressure others into behaving realistically. I remember the five-year-old boy who desperately tried to get his father to quit smoking because he was aware of all the dangers involved.

Healthy, well-adjusted gifted children, as a rule, are less often injured or involved in the destruction of property. They also often have a great deal of sensitivity and empathy for others' problems. Empathy is a kind of pressure, too, a kind of anxiety. It means that gifted children feel others' problems along with an obligation or desire to help. They have more fear of danger, more anxiety about it, because they are more aware of it. Their anxiety reflects an awareness that something needs attention. In healthy children it functions like pain, which alerts us to the fact that something is wrong. The child who discovered that the emperor had no clothes on was a gifted child with a strong sense of self. It created anxiety in him to see how everyone else was fooled, and because his self was strong, he had the strength to do something about it.

Gifted children know when a situation is unjust. If they feel strong, they will stand up for justice. The gifted often become our conscience. They are aware of the problems of the environment; seven- and eight-year-olds will organize a whole school in order to solve environmental problems. They are often the protesters. Strong gifted children do not accept the status quo. Because they do not take them for granted, they look critically at their surroundings. They insist on justice, and because they are gifted, they figure out alternatives. They will find their way out of the maze realistically and intellectually. Because gifted children think in complex terms, they often foresee problems and can keep them from happening. Their awareness of problems creates anxiety, but gifted children whose self-image is built on strength have both the courage and the ability to solve problems. It is because of this stress, created by awareness, that I believe that the gifted are our hope for saving the world.

Gifted Adults:
Their Characteristics and Emotions

Published in *Advanced Development Journal,* vol. 3 (January, 1991), pp. 81–94.

> *The gifted have their own inner agenda from which they derive great satisfaction whenever they have the opportunity to concentrate on it.*

Giftedness is a state of being—a process that makes an impact wherever it occurs. What would this world be like without our gifted adults? We cannot, of course, imagine it. Yet the gifted are not well understood, and at times are not recognized or highly regarded.

The gifted have their own inner agenda from which they derive great satisfaction whenever they have the opportunity to concentrate on it. I have spent much of my life in the company of gifted adults and their children. I have experienced and shared their emotions, actions, and reactions, and have observed how they are received by others. I have seen many of the same characteristics in gifted adults that are found in gifted children. Adult giftedness, however, has not been studied to the same extent, and therefore the gifted adult is more likely than the child to be alone in understanding his or her giftedness and in coping with the negative and positive consequences of it. This article is based on my life's work with the gifted, rather than on empirical research. I hope it will shed some light on the phenomenon of adult giftedness and enhance self-understanding in gifted adults.

Before the gifted child movement gained momentum, the gifted were perceived as the most advantaged people, those who needed no help because life contained no problems for them. It has become clear through the study of gifted children that giftedness creates a complex vision of life that brings with it a variety of reactions—both painful and joyful. There has been a tendency, partially as a reaction to the original perceptions, to look mostly at the negative aspects of giftedness. In this article, I will attempt to show not only the difficulties but also the inner exhilaration and the joy of discovery which giftedness brings. Giftedness in itself is neither a positive nor a negative factor in a person's life. It is merely a different perspective, a different way of looking at life, which can lead to the extremes of joy as well as pain.

The Impact of the Gifted on the Environment

Gifted adults are found everywhere in the world. They come from all races, ethnic backgrounds, and religions, as well as different social classes and economic circumstances. They are the inventors, the creators, the scientists. They study the past, the present, and the future. They probe the universe and the depths of the ocean. They are attracted to everything micro and macro. They give us art and music, literature, dance, and drama. They give us change, variety, and progress. They help us to interpret ourselves and the world.

The greatest impact is actually made by the vast majority of the gifted whose light does not shine on the universe, but instead penetrates our daily lives. These are the gifted teachers, parents, cooks, bus drivers, and letter writers. They are the quietly gifted—the privately gifted. Most often they're not aware of their giftedness. But the same characteristics are found in the privately gifted as in those whose contributions are more well known.

The far-reaching impact of the gifted can be either life-enhancing or life-threatening. The heart implant and the atom bomb are the result of the work of gifted people. The expansion of life and the possibility of mass destruction both require advanced knowledge and can be credited to gifted scientists. Where would we be today without Darwin or Freud or Beethoven or Shakespeare or Eleanor Roosevelt? Where would we be if there had not been Hitler? He, too, was a gifted person who had the capacity to create enormous evil. The gifted give us the best and the worst in our lives.

The Impact of the Environment on the Gifted

What is the impact of being gifted on the individuals themselves? Does being gifted create an additional burden, or does it help lift the burden of life? It does both to the extreme.

Giftedness is a burden when it has no channel for expression and it is not understood. For example, a woman I know who is mathematically and creatively gifted grew up in one of the Muslim countries where women lead very restricted lives. She felt those restrictions keenly, not as most women would, but as unbearable pain. Not only was the human being imprisoned, but also her giftedness. Her creativity needed an outlet, her mind needed to work, her understanding needed to expand. She felt choked. In her father's eyes, she did not exist. Even though she was his eldest child, he always called her younger brother his "oldest." When she came to America, she felt that for her the doors of a prison had been opened. She gained recognition for her abilities, and understanding and support for her desire to grow and learn. Her undefined discomfort changed into delight and a sense of adventure.

Not all experiences of gifted adults are so extreme, but many see their own situations as similarly restrictive. There are gifted children whose parents do not understand them; there are students who attend schools that have developed a structure which feels like stricture to them. Adults whose employment situations allow no opportunity for personal expression experience the same restrictions. In all these situations, the person's giftedness becomes a burden to him or her. This is also true in cases where people do not understand their own giftedness and misinterpret their own pressure to create and express themselves. They view their discomfort as a failing on their part. They often feel like outsiders on this earth.

Another source of constriction for the gifted arises when there is a communication gap between them and others. Many gifted individuals have no opportunity to affect the life and history of the world because circumstances in their lives close the channels of communication. A communication gap can lead to withering of the development of the gifted person. One of the best examples of this is the story of the Elephant Man, who had an illness that made him look disgusting to other people. He was mistreated and exhibited as a freak until someone found out that he was a most gifted, highly educated, and creative person. Even then, housed in a distorted body, his extraordinary abilities could not fulfill their promise.

Unsupportive environments can lead to depression, to the suppression of one's abilities, even to feelings of desperation that could become self-destructive. I also believe that when the flow of individual expression is not restricted, but instead is well received and supported, gifted adults are capable of enormous enjoyment and happiness because of their special sensitivity, depth, achievement, and discoveries.

Characteristics of the Gifted

Some time ago I wrote an article in which I listed characteristics of young gifted children (Roeper, 1988). In looking at this article I find, not surprisingly, great correlations between the personality traits of gifted children and adults. I believe that the same characteristics exist throughout life, changing somewhat as the person matures. The qualities and experiences described below are fairly typical of gifted adults.

Gifted adults differ intellectually from others.

They are more sophisticated, more global thinkers. In addition, they have the capacity to generalize. They see the complex relationships—the patterns—in the world surrounding them. They can grasp difficult concepts and phenomena. Their imagination and creativity are often incomprehensible to the average person.

Gifted adults retain childlike emotions.

Throughout their lives, the gifted are often so successful in the pursuit of their goals that they may skip some of the earlier developmental phases in which young children are confronted with the limitations reality places on them. For example, the average toddler may tumble down the stairs a few times before he learns to manage them. The gifted toddler will not attempt them until she has figured out how to keep from falling. Therefore, at times the gifted maintain a certain feeling of omnipotence because this feeling has not been challenged as much by limiting experiences in their early development.

A few gifted adults retain a type of childlike behavior that interferes with their relationships with others. I have known several brilliant, innovative people who created new directions and ideas for the institutions in which they worked. But their self-centeredness and infantile approach made it very difficult for others to work with them. Mozart is one of the best examples of the combination of genius and "childlikeness."

The ability to retain a childlike delight in discoveries and in life in general, however, can be a source of energy. Many gifted people possess the capacity to bring their giftedness to bear on their particular life circumstances to make a basic difference. At the same time, they make their situations more bearable by their ability for childlike pleasure. My uncle, Dr. Curt Bondy, a noted psychologist and prison reformer in pre-Nazi Germany, illustrates this point. He had a wonderful childlike sense of humor. He loved his car as a child loves a toy. He kept a diary in the name of the car, writing in such terms as, "Today I feel well fed. I drank thirty gallons of gasoline, but I didn't like driving in circles on the ice of the pond." Circling the pond was one of my uncle's favorite fun exercises. His enjoyment of his car was delightful to watch.

My uncle introduced "prisons without walls" in Germany in the early 1930s when this was unheard of in the rest of the world. After Hitler came to power, he founded a school where adolescent Jews could learn agriculture in order to prepare for emigration and a new life. He recognized that the greatest need for these youth was the acquisition of practical skills which they could use abroad. Many of these young people later emigrated to America and Israel and became successful farmers. This attempt to instruct young German Jews in a field that would facilitate their emigration was noteworthy in that it was done in practical and caring terms.

Along with some of his adolescent students, my uncle was taken to a concentration camp, from which he was released after a few months. Unlike most others, they all survived in good emotional and physical condition. He told me later that he consciously maintained an attitude that would not allow him or his students to see themselves as victims. He had great leadership qualities and was beloved by all these young people, as well as by his students in America and Germany.

Curt Bondy was a man who made a difference to many, many people. He could think of alternatives, such as teaching these young German Jews to become farmers, rather than despair when confronted with terrible odds. His giftedness and creative thinking abilities made his own life and the lives of these young people—as well as the lives of the prisoners he was dealing with earlier—more acceptable. It also, I am sure, gave him a certain sense of power at a time when most German Jews felt powerless. Giftedness, in this case, became his most valuable possession, one which not even the Nazis could take from him.

Gifted adults often feel fundamentally different about themselves than others feel about them.

Their potential may not be recognized by others; they may be judged only in terms of their behavior; they may be elevated in people's eyes to a point where they're not allowed to be human; they may be disparaged out of envy; or their intensity may be misunderstood as irrational. Gifted people have normal feelings of anxiety, inadequacies, and personal needs. If, however, they are in leadership positions, they often are not forgiven for their human frailties.

For example, in my position as co-founder of the Roeper City and Country School, I frequently felt that it made others feel insecure if I showed insecurities, weaknesses, or hurt feelings. My experiences were confirmed over and over again in discussions with others in leadership positions. Gifted leaders often suffer from being endowed by others with more power and ability than they really possess. This may lead to great disappointment. People want their leaders to be well and strong, which means that they may never be sick or weak. When a leader shows human frailties, people get as anxious as children do when their parents are ill. This discrepancy between the leader's expected behavior and actual humanness is difficult for the leader as well as for the community.

There is also a tendency to search for problem behavior in gifted leaders. It is as though people want to say, "They are no better than I am, after all." I have often marveled at how much effort is put into disclosing Sigmund Freud's negative qualities, as though finding these would in some way discredit his great achievements.

There are also gifted individuals who have no idea how they are perceived by others. One person in an organization had many new and forward-looking ideas but could not communicate them effectively to others, and therefore appeared opinionated. People became afraid to offer their own opinions in his presence. He had not learned to empathize with others because he lived in his own world of ideas. He did not really see himself as superior to others, but appeared as though he did. When it was pointed out to him that others felt put down by him, he said with astonishment, "I felt they just didn't respect me at all."

Gifted adults are often driven by their giftedness.

Gifted individuals do not know what creates the drive, the energy, the absolute necessity to act. They may have no choice but to explore, compose, write, paint, develop theories, educate children, conduct research, or do whatever else it is that has become uppermost in their minds. They need to know; they need to learn; they must climb the mountain because it is there. This "drivenness," this one-track-mindedness, may keep them from sleeping or eating, from engaging in sex or any other normal behavior, for the duration of their specific involvement.

I knew an artist who routinely worked day and night until his project was completed, living on black coffee, forgetting about his family around him. Everything else in his life was excluded from his consciousness during this working period. This "drivenness," of course, may also lead to personal disaster, as was the case with van Gogh and Mozart.

Creative individuals may go through cycles of ups and downs that are difficult for others to understand and cope with. Occasionally they may be forgiven by their associates for their thoughtless behavior during periods of creative stress when they have interfered with the life and work of others. For example, a drama teacher I heard of had enormous difficulties respecting the school's structure, work places, and schedule right before a performance. This often created anger and resentment in those teachers whose work and schedules had been disrupted. However, this resentment usually dissolved into admiration when they saw the results of his work with the children.

Gifted people are not as often driven to become rich, famous, or powerful. They are more likely to follow their inner agenda. I've heard people say jokingly, "If you're so smart, why aren't you rich?" The answer is, "It is because I'm so smart that I'm not rich, for that is not the goal."

Where does this drive in the gifted originate? It is in part a psychological need. It grows from the need to make sense of the world, to understand the world, to create one's own world. It is a need for mastery—intellectual, creative, physical. It probably originates from the same source that motivates people to ski down a steep hill and experience the feeling of exhilaration. It may be confrontation with and victory over death. In the last analysis, however, creative giftedness is a mystery, just as life itself is. The gift and the need to express it are both part of the person, and yet separate, just as the unborn child is a separate entity in the mother. There have been times when this force enables the sick and handicapped to carry out seemingly impossible tasks. Maybe it is because they dream the impossible dream.

Gifted adults may be overwhelmed by the pressure of their own creativity.

The gifted derive enormous satisfaction from the creative process. Much has been written about this process: how it works, the pressure of the inner agenda, the different phases it involves, the excitement and anxiety that comes with it, and the role played by the unconscious. One aspect, however, is not often mentioned.

I believe that the whole process is accompanied by a feeling of aliveness, of power, of capability, of enormous relief, and of transcendence of the limits of our own body and soul. The "unique self" flows into the world outside. It is like giving birth. Creative expression derives directly from the unique self of the creator, and its activation brings inherent feelings of happiness and aliveness, even though they may be accompanied by less positive emotions such as sadness, fear, and pain. Underneath it all is the enormous joy of discovery and personal expression. The creative experience is not unique to the gifted, but I believe that for them there are more opportunities for creativity, and that the experience is more alive and powerful.

Just as the creative process creates a feeling of happiness, the greatest unhappiness can occur if this process is interfered with or not allowed to happen. In that case, the inner pressure cannot be released. This occurs when the facilitating tools are not available, when the environment is too hostile, or when the outer or inner circumstances simply do not allow for creative expression.

Gifted adults often have strong feelings encompassing many areas of life.

They can see the foolishness of many actions in public and personal life. They see the unfairnesses and the dangers. Gifted people are more concerned with the future, and the ultimate future is death in its inevitability, finalness, and mystery.

Awareness of death exists in the young gifted child and never leaves the adult. This makes them more angry and more afraid. But gifted adults also have a heightened capacity to appreciate the beauty and the wonderment in our universe. They see the beauty of human relationships, of nature, of literature. They deeply experience the richness of the world around them; hearing beautiful music, seeing a lovely landscape, watching a child grow, observing life, feeling empathy with others. I once saw a young artist burst into tears at the sight of a beautiful Gothic cathedral. Many gifted people never lose their sense of wonderment. Because there is greater awareness, many things are felt more deeply. The ability to experience deeply is present in gifted children as well as in gifted adults (Piechowski, 1991).

Gifted adults are not necessarily popular.

They relate best to others who share their interests. They often have a small circle of friends, and sometimes only one friend, but their relationships are deep and meaningful. There also are those gifted adults whose special abilities include leadership qualities and who are an inspiration to groups, even nations.

Many gifted adults need solitude and time for contemplation and daydreaming.

Daydreaming for adults is as important as it is for children. It takes quiet time to clarify one's thoughts and feelings. Many exciting projects and ideas important to humanity had their beginnings in daydreams. However, no time for reflection is built into our modern, hectic way of life. It does not often allow for such pursuits.

Both gifted children and adults need to allow time for inner life experiences, to understand themselves, to let their inner unique self exist freely so it will not be overshadowed by stress and demands from the outside world.

Our neighbor, A.J. Levin, who was a most gifted thinker, inventor, and writer, could actually only spend a limited amount of time in the presence of others. While he found it stimulating to be with interesting company, he was most motivated by his own ideas and needed to get back to them quickly.

Gifted adults search for meaning in both the inner world and the outer world.

The need for meaning and the joy of discovering extends to discovering one's own self as well as the world around one. Many gifted people who have achieved a great deal in the world still can never overcome a feeling of dissatisfaction, of a need unfulfilled, until they truly experience their own unique self. Often this is a matter of removing layers of accumulated attempts to live up to outside expectations which are foreign to their inner reality. Only through careful and honest exploration, alone or with a friend or through counseling, can this inner tension be resolved. Often, too, creativity is not free to express itself until this work has been done.

A young teacher I knew serves as an example. She was often at odds with parents and other teachers. In the classroom, however, where she had a great deal of freedom to develop her own program, her results were spectacular. She inspired the children to do the most beautiful artwork. She developed exciting science and social studies projects. The children felt drawn to her warm acceptance of them. She could create her own world in the classroom, but she could not really connect with the world of adults. Although she tried hard to adjust, she didn't succeed. She felt inferior in the outside world. Through therapy she discovered the unconscious reasons for her feelings and learned that she had a right to be herself and to expect respect and understanding. She had found herself. This made it possible for her to see others as they really were. Her changed attitude created change in the responses of those around her.

Gifted adults often develop their own method of learning and of grasping concepts.

This may lead to conflict with others who don't understand the route used by the gifted person to solve a problem. Just as children surprise their math teachers because they reach the correct conclusion by a process unknown to the teacher and often unknown to themselves, some adults use approaches puzzling to others. There are occasions when a more complicated or more sophisticated route leads to even better results than the usual method.

For example, at the Roeper City and Country School we had a fleet of buses that picked up the children. The routes had to be carefully worked out each year. Some of the drivers realized that a longer route might actually be quicker since there would be less traffic. Others could not think along such lines. The fact that unusual thinking is often not comprehended may keep the more sophisticated and more reasonable action from happening.

There are also ways of dealing with daily problems that could be described as the "educated guess" or as something that arises from the unconscious. I believe that many experiences add up to certain insights in gifted people's minds even without their being aware of the logical sequence. Their accumulated knowledge leads to their actions, but they may not be able to trace the origins of their decisions. My husband and I have experienced this many times in our understanding of children. We have incorporated into our unconscious our long experience of living with gifted children. It has often astonished other people that we may see a child for a few minutes and discover a characteristic just from this brief observation—from the child's behavior or expression or language—without being able to tell what led to the discovery and without using testing devices.

Many gifted teachers and parents have the capacity of empathy. They know in an instant what upsets a particular child, what words she needs to hear and how she thinks and learns. Others miscommunicate because they do not have these unconscious "clues." Through this type of empathic knowing, Helen Keller's teacher, Anne Sullivan, was able to find the clue to reaching her famed student. This unconscious reaction, however, requires the inner freedom to believe in one's intuition rather than in conventional wisdom.

Not all gifted persons allow themselves to listen to their inner voice. Those who have the freedom and the capacity to follow their own drummer experience a feeling of power and inner achievement. It is difficult for them to understand that others do not see their logic. Less gifted people are more apt to see the logic of the moment rather than the complex impact of their actions or the eventual implications for the future. For example, struggling organizations may decide to cut their mailing lists in order to save money, while a gifted person might want to consider the fact that this limits the organization's exposure and inevitably leads to further decline.

Gifted adults have a special problem awareness.

This means that they have the ability to predict consequences, see relationships, and foresee problems that are likely to occur. This ability leads to greater anxiety and concerns, but also may lead to the prevention of foreseeable problems through finding innovative solutions.

In running the Roeper School, I often kept a problem from developing because I saw conditions that would make it a likely possibility. However, I would get no recognition for doing this because no one else knew that its potential existed. I would, for instance, suggest that a certain child not be placed in a group with a certain teacher because I knew that there would be a personality clash. Or, to put it positively, I would know that a certain child would thrive with a particular teacher. On occasions when I was overruled by others, my inner predictions would often come true.

Gifted adults are able to see patterns of development and growth, and therefore will recognize trends.

This allows them to predict and, by certain actions, to influence the trend. For example, my husband, George, developed a fairly accurate method for predicting enrollment at our school for a given year. He analyzed the enrollment trends of previous years and developed a formula from them. Some of the people who entered the data did not understand the underlying concept: namely, that if there are a certain number of applications in January, one can predict a certain definable increase in the spring, which becomes smaller in the summer. The sum of these factors predicts the approximate number of students who will be enrolled in a particular school year. Early in the year, therefore, one can more or less "guess" what the enrollment will be and base budget decisions on this estimate—unless, of course, something unforeseen happens, such as an economic downturn.

As far as we know, after we retired from the school this formula was not used again, and mistaken predictions were made which then led to errors in the development of the budget. Unfortunately, the gifted are able to predict trends, but are not likely trendsetters because it is difficult to convince others of their way of thinking.

Gifted adults often react angrily to being subjected to public relations methods of image-making.

Just as gifted children notice and react when teachers pretend to know more than they actually do, gifted adults react with anger when they are exposed to any kind of propaganda or slanted reporting, whether it is in politics or in daily life. It offends their sense of justice.

Inherent in giftedness, I truly believe, is a demanding search for truth. There are, of course, those gifted adults who are themselves the type who manipulate the truth, and unfortunately they might be very successful.

Gifted adults are perfectionists.

This leads to basic differences in their behavior and reactions. They are perfectionists in terms of their own standards and expectations, not necessarily in terms of the expectations of the outside world. There is an inner urge to fulfill their own expectations even if no one else sees the need to do so. They feel very guilty if they cannot carry out what they expect from themselves. Many cannot stand injustice and feel compelled to stand up for their beliefs, whatever they are. If they embrace a moral behavior, they probably will not deviate from it. This trait may lead to the appearance of rigidity.

I must use myself as an example here, because I think it shows this tendency very well and was, in fact, a puzzle to me until I understood its origin. Our school was very successful in the early years, when our approach was a more traditional one. It was geared to the expectations of society and expected children to perform in the traditional mold. All this took place within a humanistic framework. We tried to help individual children make a good adjustment to expectations by giving them personal support and empathy. Child psychology and knowledge of unconscious motivation were always part of our educational process. However, the goal at that time was for the child's adjustment to outside expectations rather than the development of a framework which would include the child's own inner agenda and resources.

Even though things went well, I felt that we were not fulfilling our promise to children, and this in turn created a growing sense of guilt in me. I began to look for an alternate structure to facilitate children's development of the unique self and, at the same time, build a bridge toward society's expectations. Many gifted adults cannot find that "connection," that bridge. My only motivation was the feeling that the education we provided was not perfect—not giving children what they truly needed.

When I finally discovered the open classroom and all of its possibilities, I felt a great sense of satisfaction and release. Introducing the open classroom was not easy at first. It resulted in unhappy teachers and the withdrawal of some students from the school. From that perspective, the innovation was not a positive one. From my perspective, it was necessary to open a new door for the growth of the children. Our innovative approach to education, which seemed to make children feel safe and challenged, later became the specific attraction of the school. My motivation did not come from the outside and was not based on approval by others and society, but solely on the desire to create an approach which would allow children to become the persons they really were. Once the change had been made, it became obvious to teachers and parents that it was a positive one (Roeper, 1990).

Gifted adults are often confronted with the problem of having too many abilities in too many areas in which they would like to work, discover, and excel.

For example, university students often move from one field of study to another because they are attracted to both. They may at times end up not doing well in either. However, other gifted students have a great capacity for learning and may be able to study several areas side by side and acquire several doctorates in fields far removed from each other.

Some gifted students have the amazing capacity to do several things at the same time—such as watch television, play chess, and study—and do them all well.

Gifted adults often have feelings of being misunderstood, of being outsiders, and of being unable to communicate.

This may be the most difficult problem confronting the gifted. They may accept traditional expectations as their own standards and then feel inferior because their inner drives lead somewhere else.

Einstein once wrote in a letter to his sister that he was depressed because he felt he failed his parent's expectations (Dukas & Hoffmann, 1979). On the other hand, as he grew older he became one of those who create their own forum, their own framework into which others will fit. Such people are able to make their dream penetrate the reality of their environment, whether it is by directing an orchestra, developing a laboratory, founding a school, or nurturing the growth of a business. This involves much responsibility and many problems; it may lead to failure or success, but it provides a continuing basis for personal expression with fewer restraints.

It is true that there are always pressures from the outside that intrude on freedom. These pressures are, of course, necessary realities. However, if the gifted person has a strong self-image, intrusion from the outside will actually be stimulating. Other gifted adults create in isolation, such as artists, writers, and scientists. Isolation, although it may entail problems, permits free development toward one's own goals and brings with it the unhindered enjoyment of one's own creativity.

Gifted adults have difficulty understanding the seemingly inconsistent and short-sighted behavior of others.

They may feel helpless to deal with such behavior. Any kind of confrontation creates problems with many gifted people because few issues are clear-cut and they can usually see both sides rather than absolute good or bad, right or wrong. They are aware that everything is relative, depending on one's perspective. And yet they often come to believe in a basic universal morality which is based on a reverence for life and beauty.

Gifted adults perceive a difference between justice and equality.

This may mean that at times they will make decisions that seem unfair to others. They understand consistency in a different manner. This view grows out of a long-range, deeper vision of the complexities, while others may base their decisions on a narrow sense of fairness.

It is an injustice, for example, to provide equal educational experiences for all children regardless of their abilities. Six-year-olds who are capable of reading on what is considered third-grade level should have access to suitable literature, and those who cannot read need careful instruction at a different level.

Gifted adults may find it more difficult than others to take risks because they realize more what is at stake.

This applies to physical daring as well as the risk of disagreeing with the majority on issues of justice. At the same time, the gifted may understand the need for risk-taking more deeply and end up involved in the more dangerous action, possibly with greater anxiety and only after more careful investigation. As a rule, it will take the gifted longer to decide to dive into the pool, but they will be less likely to hit their heads on the bottom.

One of the most outstanding features of gifted adults is their sense of humor.

It takes complex thinking to see the funny side of life. The sense of humor of the gifted differs from that of other people. It often consists of subtle jokes, intricate teasing, or puns. Gifted people often find that their jokes are received with silence because they are not understood.

Gifted adults can develop emotional problems related to their abilities, but they also have greater resources for dealing with their problems.

The gifted commonly experience inner conflicts that differ in nature and degree from those of others (Piechowski, 1991). These conflicts are often connected with feelings of guilt for not having lived up to their own expectations, compounded with feelings of disappointment, panic, and the complete lack of power, and the use of their creativity to conjure up the worst scenario. These feelings may grow out of an inability to truly make sense of their own lives. However, the gifted also have a greater capacity to listen to themselves, work through problems, and find ways to heal themselves.

The gifted often have difficulties with authority figures.

They are independent thinkers and do not automatically accept the decisions of their supervisors. Their reactions may be based on their perceptions of the fallibility of decisions, or they may relate to moral questions. Gifted employees are often driven to take actions against situations they don't approve of, and therefore become threatening to people in authority. Gifted people function well in a participatory community or with supervisors who are also gifted and can accept their attitudes and innovations. One comment I heard often from our teachers was that they liked working with us at our school because their creativity was respected and their job was not threatened even if they disagreed with us.

If their natural tendency to question authority is dealt with too harshly in childhood, some gifted individuals become permanently alienated from society and resort to criminal behavior. Gifted individuals who are not living in an environment that allows for their unusual need for self-growth and creative expression may resort to antisocial behavior in their search for an outlet for their inner creative pressures. When the gifted become misdirected, they are more dangerous to society because they are more capable of deception. For this reason, I believe that gifted education needs to stress the moral development of children.

Many gifted people have strong moral convictions and try to use their specific talents, insights, and knowledge for the betterment of the world.

These are the people who, for example, use their gifts in the service of the planet. It is the gifted who are global thinkers, who have an understanding of the complexities, the patterns, and the interrelatedness of global affairs. It is the gifted who have the capacity to replace the world's short-sighted, short-term reactions with careful, overall solutions. A combination of a deep commitment to our planet and the ability to cope with it is our only hope for survival. Eleanor Roosevelt's work with the United Nations exemplifies the impact that a gifted individual can have on the world. Unfortunately, the world's lack of understanding of the gifted prevents more of them from fully developing their potential to help society.

Conclusion

Giftedness is an ongoing process and not a product. The process leads in a direction that differs from the direction of the majority, but which also can integrate with it and bring about change. It can lead to the greatest wretchedness and the highest ecstasy. The gifted person has the capacity to penetrate the complexities of the landscape of life and understand its supreme interconnectedness. Experiencing one's own giftedness—one's creative abilities—is one of the most exciting aspects of the gifted person's life.

References

Dukas, H., & Hoffmann, B. *Albert Einstein: The Human Side.* Princeton, NJ: Princeton University Press, 1979.

Piechowski, M.M. "Emotional Development and Emotional Giftedness." In N. Colangelo & G.A. Davis (Eds.), *Handbook of Gifted Education.* Boston: Allyn & Bacon, 1991, pp. 285-306.

Roeper, A. "Identifying the Young Gifted Child." *Parents' Press,* 9 (1), 1, 4 (1988).

—*Educating Children for Life: The Modern Learning Community.* Monroe, NY: Trillium, 1990.

Participatory vs. Hierarchical Models for Administration: The Roeper School Experience

Published in *The Roeper Review*, vol. 9, no. 1 (September, 1986), pp. 4–10.

There is in our society a pervasive acceptance of a hierarchy among human beings. Teachers are considered more right than children, and influential parents more right than teachers. In a structure that grows out of a deep belief in equal human rights, these unfair assumptions disappear.

It is usually assumed that the functioning of a school is determined by the people who head the school. This, of course, is true to a large extent. The role of administrators, although varied, is crucial to any educational endeavor. Their tasks and job descriptions differ widely, depending upon the particular situation. Many variants, including the size of the school system and whether the school is public or private, affect the role of administrators.

Principals or heads of schools are the leaders of school communities or educational institutions. They interpret a school's philosophy, establish priorities based on short- or long-term goals, initiate plans, and innovate programs. They are not only catalysts for innovation but also mediators between different factions of the school community. They are executives, financial officers, public relations officers, program directors, and even parents. They also act as the focus of the conflicting needs and demands of the people in the institution.

As such, principals can easily lose their own perspective and identity. Some survive in their positions only by becoming human weather vanes, turned by the wind that blows the strongest. Yet what is needed the most from them is true leadership that can be articulated in many ways. Amazingly, and to their credit, there are many heads of schools who remain true to themselves in the midst of this diversity of demands and who evolve as individuals whose personalities make a dramatic impact on a particular educational community.

What are the factors that determine the differences between one principal and another? What determines their individual goals and priorities, their modes of implementation, and ultimately, their visions? Several factors certainly influence an administrative style, including the types of families involved in the school, the staff, the economic and political climate of the society at large, and the community in which the school is located. It is the combination of these influences and the personality and motivations of the principal that determine the unique character of a school. This atmosphere, as it evolves historically, shapes the style of leadership exerted by each new administrator. However, the most influential factor affecting the style of leadership is the prevailing philosophy of the school community and its existing structure.

School Philosophy and Administrative Style

In my opinion, there are two fundamentally different philosophies of education that determine the role of principals. Within these two philosophies, which I will describe at some length below, there are variations, different structures for implementation, different individual approaches, and, to be sure, combinations of both philosophies. Each of these approaches makes a strong but different impact on children, especially on gifted children.

Education for Success

The first educational philosophy, and by far the more prevalent, is education for success. This approach is achievement- and product-oriented. The process is based on particular teaching methods, and its implementation structure is hierarchical. It can be visually represented as a pyramidal structure with children at the bottom, principals on the top, and teachers and department heads somewhere in between.

In the education for success philosophy, children move up through the grades. All are expected to learn the same things at the same time, in the same way, and at the same age. Motivation for learning is based on a competitive system supported by grades. Awards are given to signal approval, and punishment is meted out to signal disapproval. Children are evaluated on the basis of their success or failure in subject matter only, which is structured in a sequential, linear manner. They are viewed as passive learners, as vessels waiting to be filled. One of the goals of this model of education is to function within the existing norms of the larger culture and its expectations, to acknowledge the status quo and make children succeed within its parameters.

Education for Life

The second model of education is education for life. This philosophy is based on the concept of self-actualization and entails learning by experience, discovery, exploration, active involvement, and creative expression. Individual children are viewed as unique, not judged by the norm. The process of learning is based on knowledge of characteristics of the individual and his or her developmental phases as well as patterns of growth. Learning is seen as an activity: Children bring themselves to the process and make the material their own, changing it while incorporating it into their unique personalities. Emphasis is placed on learning and on methods of teaching that can be adapted to this goal.

This model assumes that individual children learn in different ways, with different timing and different interests. Expectations are based on the individual realities and the particular stage of development of each child. Emphasis is placed on cooperation in diversity, rather than competition within sameness. Subject matter is learned in a global, experiential manner rather than a sequential, linear one. Skills are learned as tools for self-mastery. The goal is the total growth of the child, with the view that he or she will make an impact on the world.

The education for life model differs radically from the education for success model. The latter grows out of the belief that people are defined by their skills, that they are what they do and how well they do it. The former, by contrast, stems from the belief that people are defined by their unique selves. Emphasis is placed on the growth of the self and mastery of the environment.

Impact of Philosophy on Administration

Traditionally, most education has been conceived on the education for success model. Institutions of modern education are structured largely on this basis. Most people take this approach for granted and judge all others against it. Education for life and self-mastery, although not without historical precedent, has become popular only recently and is often viewed with skepticism.

Pressure is put on the education for life model to prove itself in terms of the more generally accepted education for success model. Feeling this pressure has always placed constraints on administrators and educators who pursue this second philosophy. As a result, some programs that purport to be based on an education for life philosophy actually model themselves on the education for success model. But even these hybrids have developed new methods as a result of the education for life model, and children have been given the opportunity to learn and grow in different ways in many institutions. Individualized, nongraded, and open education are only a few of the fruits that blossomed from this effort.

One generally accepted norm is that the administrative structure of any educational institution is based on the concept of "hierarchy." Therefore, the most obvious way in which education for life has adapted to the norm (or has never moved away from it) is by accepting a hierarchical administrative structure. Most, but not all, of these programs use some variant of a hierarchical structure as the basis of their administration, thus creating a dichotomy between the operation of the school and its philosophy. When the goal is to help children learn how to create and participate in their own destinies, a contradiction presents itself in their learning environment if their teachers function in a top-down hierarchical structure. This dichotomy has become obvious to some educators in charge of programs for gifted children, who characteristically desire to understand and participate in decisions that concern them. A number of programs have drawn the conclusion that a participatory structure creates a community that allows all of its members to make an impact on their collective destiny and is more in line with the education for life philosophy. As a result, some fundamentally different administrative structures that redefine the role of leadership have been created.

The Roeper School Experience

The Roeper City and Country School, which was founded by my husband George Roeper and me, is based on the education for life philosophy. The changes that occurred at our school during our tenure as its leaders can serve as an example of the impact created by some changes in the structure of administration. In this case, the leadership, the staff, and the children remained unchanged while we moved first to a new educational model and then to a different administrative one.

In the following paragraphs, I will describe the history of our philosophy and how it developed and crystallized over the years, as well as our attempt to implement new educational principles and administrative structures. I will also describe how our experiences over the years changed our style of leadership.

The structure and philosophy of the Roeper City and Country School have their origins in my husband's and my childhood and youth, which was spent in Germany in a boarding school run by my parents, Drs. Max and Gertrud Bondy, before and during the devastating experiences of the early Hitler years. The specific character of our school was formed by our humanistic philosophy, our German-Jewish culture, and our subsequent integration into our new homeland. From my mother, a psychoanalyst, we brought with us the legacy of seeing the emotional development of children as a major ingredient in the educational process. From my father, an art historian and educator, we gained a tremendous sense of community and an emphasis on philosophy, art, and culture. Our interest in gifted children grew out of our observation that they had become educationally disadvantaged in America and our sense that they might be the ones who would have the capacity to someday improve the condition of the world.

Ours was one of the first integrated schools; we have always been happy about the fact that our school looked like a United Nations in miniature, for its population consisted of children from all different ethnic, racial, cultural, and religious backgrounds. It was our intention to create a world in miniature, for we believed that the principles that govern relations between nations must also govern relations within the school community.

We wanted to create a school community that would teach children the skills of cooperation and give them an understanding of interdependence, not simply teach them how to live in a hierarchy-based society and its underlying notions of victory and defeat and climbing up the ladder of success. We wanted to create opportunities for children to learn how to influence their own destinies as well as accept responsibility for their actions. Gifted children have great awareness of the problems of the world and their immediate environment, and at an early age they understand the difference between obedience and responsibility.

We wanted to develop an educational program which reflected all of these principles. This meant that equal emphasis had to be placed on emotional, intellectual, creative, social, and physical development. These needed to be seen as one integrated unit designed to support the unique growth of each child. We sought a flexible program that valued individual differences, characteristics, and needs. Over the years, we experimented with different systems until we arrived at the one that seemed the most appropriate to our philosophy. Originally, we began with an approach that, although traditional in nature, was still flexible. Children moved from grade to grade, sat at their individual desks, and followed a prescribed, uniform curriculum. Even at that time our philosophy was reflected in this framework. Much emphasis was placed on areas not conventionally part of the academic curriculum, such as music, drama, dancing, and current events. The developmental phases— the psychology of child development—were always the basis of our perceptions of the child. Our style of leadership at that time was traditional, however.

Even though we always tried to be empathetic and respectful of people's needs and listened to their points of view, there was no formal participation in the manner in which decisions were reached. There was no organized structure of input, although our doors were always open. As the heads of the school, we held final and complete responsibility for all major decisions. The structure was hierarchical and included different levels of power. This automatically ascribed a specific role to each member of the community, but the staff was ultimately dependent on us. In most cases, the staff was confident that our decisions were just and fair. In some respects, the atmosphere of the school in those days resembled that of a family.

Especially as more younger staff members were hired, we increasingly became parental figures to many in the community. At times there was a kind of sibling rivalry between staff members; there were always those who felt they had more access to us than others, which gave them a certain kind of power. Along with these parent-child relationships came some unrealistic expectations. This, too, was the inevitable consequence of a hierarchical structure, and many people in similar structures experience this result. It is, in fact, one of the reasons people are attracted to the structure of hierarchy. It relieves them of the burden and anxiety of making decisions and taking responsibility. It also implies that where others have power to make decisions, they also have the obligation to solve all problems that result from them.

At times, resentments developed when our human limitations kept us from fulfilling some unrealistic expectations, or when the complexity of problems made it necessary to leave the wishes of some unfulfilled. Children are initially in this position of dependency, until they grow into independent adults who must return to a new form of dependency in hierarchical structures. For all of these reasons, we felt that our educational program and the surrounding framework of its administrative structure did not quite fulfill our promise to children or to other members of the community concerning the philosophy of the school itself.

We began to feel more and more that there was a dichotomy between the philosophy and our interpretation of it. Much as we tried to focus on the development of individual children in terms of preparing them for life, not just for college, our priorities still reflected an orientation toward traditional success according to the school's community structure. This expressed itself in many ways. For example, an eight-year-old, who was also a daydreamer, did not cover the expected curriculum by the end of the school year. His parents worried over this, and his teachers pressured him into fulfilling their demands. Everyone was aware that this was a gifted child who was excited and knowledgeable about understanding the physical environment. He was also concerned about his parents' impending separation. Although we often talked about how each child needed to be allowed to grow at his own rate and in his own way, the child was confronted with the disappointment of his parents and teachers when he did not fulfill the norms of the traditional curriculum. He was made to feel that he was failing and that his interest in the environment, which would be covered in the next grade's curriculum, somehow did not count as much as learning to spell correctly.

We wondered why this was happening. We began to suspect that it was caused by the traditional program of the school, which included regular achievement tests and standard academic expectations. The more we became aware of the characteristics of gifted children, the more we felt that conventional expectations were geared to norms which did not fit them. They were simply not based on the characteristics of these children and their manner of growth and development. In fact, we wondered whether the traditional approach actually met the needs of most children, gifted or not. We wondered, too, whether there might be other structures of education that would allow children to develop more freely. We began looking for a system in which, for instance, children's interests in the environment, as in the case mentioned above, would be highly valued, and their problems with spelling would be acknowledged but not judged.

Consequently, we tried an ungraded program in which children were grouped according to skill level rather than age. This was somewhat more appropriate because it allowed children to grow at their own rate rather than follow arbitrary expectations, but it was still geared to the same goals. Finally, we became acquainted with the British model of the integrated day school and felt that we had at last found a useful approach to education for life. Out of this model we developed our own open classroom approach.

What follows is a description of the structure of our school at the time of our retirement in 1980. In many ways the school still functions in the same manner today, but I can best describe the period during which I served as its head.

The Program

The Roeper City and Country School enrolled gifted children of preschool through high school age. There was close cooperation between the school and the surrounding public schools. In fact, many of our students were recommended by public school teachers. The program was geared to the needs and characteristics of gifted children. I was in charge of the lower school, and my husband George was in charge of the high school.

Grouping

In the Roeper City and Country School's open classroom approach, children were grouped according to principles that differed from those of conventional schools. The lower school was divided into three stages. Stage II consisted of approximately three- to seven-year-olds, Stage III of approximately seven- to eight-year-olds, and Stage IV of nine- to twelve-year-olds. Each group therefore contained several ages and grade levels.

There were many reasons for this. One was that children learn and grow at different rates, and age grouping does not necessarily accommodate their skill level. We set specific goals for each child based on his or her individual characteristics, needs, and interests. Another reason for groupings with various ages was that we did not believe in the lockstep movement of children from grade to grade, since, realistically, goals cannot be equal for all children. We wanted our children to understand that all human beings have equal value, and that being older or in a higher grade does not make one a better person. We were flexible about making changes. A child might be placed in a group at the beginning of the year, but if for some reason that placement did not seem to be working out, he or she could be moved to another group after a consultation that involved the parents, the child, and the teachers.

Special Classes

One unique feature of the school was a partial homeroom system to which was attached an extensive system of special classes, open to children from different groups. In other words, not all children from the same group always had the same special class together. They selected a special class and met children from other groups. This system changed in structure as the child moved from stage to stage. I will describe this more fully later on.

Tasks of the Homeroom Teacher

Our staff's diversity of teaching styles was part of our assets and increased the possibility of matching the specific needs of a given child with the specific strengths of a particular teacher. Homeroom teachers were responsible for children's growth in language, the arts, math, and social studies. They also functioned as counselors to the children. Together, teachers and students created a classroom learning environment in which the children were academically, physically, and emotionally involved.

Children need personal attention in the midst of group interaction. Therefore, we created opportunities for teachers to work with children individually, in small groups, or in large groups. Children also need to experience satisfying results. They need help in planning and following through tasks even, and most especially, when they result in failure. They need to understand that learning includes taking risks and persevering. Children are born with a motivation to learn about and master their environment. Our students learned skills for mastery rather than for grades. All children want independent work appropriate to their individual interests and needs. This requires an awareness on the part of the teachers. Through regular meetings with individual children and by reading what they had written in journals, teachers knew what each child was doing.

Children need a teacher of their own, even though they may not spend all day with that teacher. It is necessary that they know that "their" teacher is there to help them when they are unable to help themselves. This may mean planning with children and insisting that their commitments be fulfilled. I would like to emphasize this last point particularly, for some people feel that it is against the basic nature of the open classroom to put pressure on children in any way. Actually, the open classroom is based on the notion that structure serves the philosophy of the educational environment. It does *not* mean to not group, not schedule, not force, and never demand. It means, rather, that these things must be done in terms of the needs of individual children or the group rather than in terms of artificial, external requirements unrelated to the individual or the group. In many cases, external demands and internal needs coincide.

The role of the teacher in this system was different from the role of the teacher in the hierarchical tradition. Our teachers provided a living and learning environment that included all types of opportunities for individualized learning, skill- and concept-learning, experiential learning, and group discussions and projects. Our teachers were also concerned about the creative expression of each individual child and his or her emotional and social growth. The open classroom, with its unique physical arrangement and educational structure, made it possible for children to interact with one another throughout the school day. Teachers were faced with the task of building bridges between the unique characteristics and needs of individual students and the demands and expectations of the outside world. Because of the amount of mutual respect that developed from this structure, teachers became the children's allies. In this atmosphere, children felt protected by their teachers and grew and learned freely. They dared to take the necessary risks to widen their personal worlds.

Within this structure, teachers also had the task of coordinating special classes. One of the important skills that children need to learn, and usually have little opportunity to learn, is the skill of making choices. At the Roeper City and Country School, the opportunity to make choices began with the youngest child. In the Stage II group, one hour each day was set aside for activities outside the classroom. Each child had an opportunity to participate in one of a variety of different activities. Special teachers in science, math, music, physical education, and other subjects were available at different times of the day, and the library was always open. Such classes were offered on a scheduled basis to each learning group so that the children would have a basis for selection.

The special classes were particularly important for gifted children because many of them had special gifts in areas that would have been impossible for their homeroom teachers to fulfill. This also created the opportunity for children from different learning groups to mingle with one another and to become acquainted with and attached to a number of adults.

The same principles existed in the Stage III group, but because these children had reached a different stage of development, they were able to make a six-week commitment to spend each afternoon at one of these different subject areas. Stage IV offered its students a wide variety of choices for activities and classes that were available at different times of the day. Often, different areas within a single subject area were offered. Students had a greater number of choices, some of which grew out of their particular interests. In this way, they became actively involved in their education.

Students usually called teachers by their first names and felt free to disagree with them. Since the teachers were viewed as human beings, they could freely admit mistakes without losing face. This was particularly important, because it was always possible that a given child would have knowledge in a certain field that the teacher lacked. This never minimized the leadership role of teachers as long as they were truly capable, knowledgeable, and enthusiastic people who also viewed themselves as learners who were committed to their children.

As the children became more and more able to participate in their destinies, the dichotomy between our approach to education and our administrative structure became evident. The staff needed to be able to make a real impact on the school for the sake of justice and to be models for the children. Many of us realized that the current administrative structure was not in keeping with the philosophy of the school.

Administrators and staff found themselves moving more and more in the direction of changing the school's approach to administration. We entered uncharted territory with no model to follow. We called the new model a "participatory democracy" or "flattened hierarchy." A type of hierarchy still continued because of the existing board structure under which the school was operated. We, the heads, had final decision-making power within the school.

However, we were able to develop a new participatory process within this existing governmental framework. Most importantly, we all learned to think in nonhierarchical terms. It became more and more clear that the process that led to a decision was as important as the decision itself. The participatory approach was based on the principle that everyone who would be affected by a decision would have the opportunity to be involved in the process that led to the final decision. The initiation of this participatory process created changes that affected every aspect of the school community, including its board of trustees.

Changes in Administrative Practice

It was decided that one student, one alumnus, and two people from either the teaching or the support staff would become voting members of the school's board of trustees. The staff members and students were appointed by the board from a pool of several candidates who had been nominated by the staff.

Within the school there were many different ways in which the staff participated on a more regular basis in planning and decision making. Teachers worked as a team in each stage. Determining what each stage would entail was their common responsibility. Each child became known to many adults: the homeroom teachers, assistant and special teachers, and the previous year's teachers. Homeroom and special teachers met regularly to discuss individual children's development. Children could be moved at any time from one homeroom to another, or from one stage to another, after consultation with the child and his or her parents. Differences of teaching style and emphasis were openly discussed and used as criteria for original placement or change. Children who exhibited behavioral problems in one environment often found a comfortable niche in another. There were several meetings with parents during the year, at which the child was often present. Written reports were handled differently in each stage. At the end of each year, careful placement was made by the entire group of teachers. Children might remain in the same group for one, two, or three years, or they might be moved into another group within that stage or to a new stage altogether.

The teams of teachers planned the programs for each unit in all respects. They set up rules, guidelines, and procedures and concerned themselves with the issues of the moment, whether about academic procedures, racial awareness issues, sex education, relationships between younger and older students, or concerns that related to the needs of teachers or the school as a whole. Each stage was semi-autonomous and had a structure based on its students' developmental needs.

Benefits Committee

We also formed a benefits committee which consisted of teaching staff, support staff, and administration. All matters of staff concern such as salary, sick leaves, medical insurance, and so on were discussed and then sent as proposals to the board or, if more appropriate, referred to other internal committees when problems remained unsolved by the benefits committee itself. This is the exact opposite method of conflict resolution that one would find in a union. Our focus was on cooperation, whereas unions are usually based on confrontation.

Administrative Councils

We also formed administrative councils, one for the lower school and one for the upper school. These two groups met periodically and in combined meetings. In the lower school, the administrative council consisted of the administrators and coordinators of each stage. These meetings were open to anyone who was interested in attending them. Those who were most likely to be affected by a decision were the most likely to attend. The staff also participated in staff evaluation, hiring, firing, enrollment, and many other areas. Some of these areas I would like to describe in greater detail so that the ways in which they differed from the traditional methods of educational settings will become more evident.

Teacher Evaluation

One of the participatory areas was teacher evaluation. Traditionally, the head of the school evaluated its teachers and determined hiring, rehiring, and firing practices. These decisions were based on the administrator's personal observations, with possible input from official encounters with division or department heads, informal experiences with teachers, or pressure from various groups. We discontinued this practice completely and instead developed a committee with a very careful evaluation structure. Evaluations now included specific observation periods by members of the committee (chosen by me as head of the lower school), by volunteers, and also by the person who was to be evaluated. At times, as in the case of a specialist on subjects such as music or art, outside experts were also invited to participate. Questionnaires would be sent to parents. All of this was carefully discussed beforehand with the person who was being evaluated. The committee took all the collected materials and came to conclusions that I then would discuss with the individual. These evaluations often led to surprising insights and sometimes disproved casual perceptions of the person. By means of this structure, the perceptions of less outspoken members of the community became known; the most vocal people were not always in the majority.

The evaluation process was perhaps the most difficult change that was introduced at our school, and it required a degree of open-mindedness on the part of all. Once the process had been decided upon by everybody, the need for peer loyalty no longer existed and was replaced by loyalty to the community. This could happen only with the trust that developed in the evaluation structure itself. It was most difficult, however, to develop this changed attitude. There were many times when all of us would lapse into former ways of thinking about and doing things, and this would make it difficult to carry out our newer purposes. As a whole, however, the new structure created more openness and was more acceptable to the people who were evaluated than previous methods had been. Most people developed a new sense of security, knowing that decisions would be based on a broader and fairer evaluation. And if, for instance, a staff member was asked to leave after a very careful evaluation, it would not as easily create a sense of insecurity in the others who otherwise might wonder if they would be next.

Hiring

Another area in which the staff became involved was the hiring of new staff members. This was done through group interviews after I had selected a number of suitable candidates and they had all spent time visiting the school and, whenever possible, teaching or working in the classroom for a brief period. Again, as in the process of enrollment, hiring, and evaluation, the process and end results were owned by all. Some of these practices exist in other schools, but not as part of the structure; rather, the process tends to depend on the benevolence of individual administrators.

Enrollment

Teachers also participated in the enrollment process, which evolved over the years. It was important to all of us that children fit into our specific environment and that their parents agree with our approach to education. Each prospective student visited a classroom for a whole day. The parents filled out a lengthy questionnaire and had an initial interview with an administrator. An IQ test was administered to the child, not as a screening device, but as one more factor to be considered in his or her total profile. This was followed by an evaluation. The applicants then met different teachers. At the same time, an administrator spoke with the parents as a group to become more acquainted with them. All of the information about whether a particular child would be appropriate for our school was gathered and considered by the staff as a whole. In this way, objective as well as subjective information was gathered.

The responsibility for accepting a child for enrollment was shared by many. Rather than having no choice in the matter, teachers made a commitment to the child from the beginning. There were many cases in which teachers decided to accept a child with problems because they felt a desire to help him or her. Often they succeeded. Had they just been confronted with the child, they might have resented it and not become as involved in supporting the child's specific needs.

Relationships with Parents

The atmosphere of openness also brought about a subtle change in the relationship between parents and the school. Many parents already saw themselves as part of the community and participated cooperatively. However, certain attitudes now became official policy. Since teachers were no longer seen as teachers only, but also as human beings, it was acceptable if they did not succeed with every child. The parents felt freer to express their concerns, and these were discussed openly.

Prior to this, parents who had a criticism about a particular teacher would voice their concerns to me privately and then ask me to rectify the situation. As a rule, they did not want to be identified to the teacher. Nothing is more disturbing and less helpful to a teacher than to be told by an administrator that people are saying certain things about him or her, or that there is a rumor that something in his or her teaching is remiss, when the teacher does not know the context in which this concern evolved. We insisted that people take responsibility for their perceptions, and I often functioned as a facilitator in disagreements between parents and teachers. It was interesting to see how parents developed techniques to be honest without also becoming hostile, and how teachers became secure enough to cope with those instances without becoming threatened or afraid.

The Role of the Administrator

The role of my husband and me as heads of the school changed. From being the top of the hierarchy, we became the facilitators of various group processes. We saw ourselves as responsible for the success of this new process of administration. Our tasks included learning and teaching others how to be equal members of the community. We saw our area of expertise as the overview of the entire school, while each staff member was the expert in his or her own area. The information gleaned from these various sources informed decisions that affected everyone.

I cannot adequately describe all of the changes that took place in all of us and in the life of the Roeper City and Country School during the time when I was one of its leaders. Often these were the result of subtle occurrences in daily life, yet they were very significant to the structure as a whole. It was difficult, even frightening, for some of the staff to understand that we, as heads of the school, did not have the power to provide absolute security for them, nor could we accept responsibility for everything that happened as a consequence of their decisions. We all had to learn that chances for security are greater when we all work together openly. For some, it was difficult to give up the concept of seeing us as parents and replace this with a concept of us as friends, facilitators, and experts in the overall administration of the school.

There were practical problems as well. The process was very time-consuming to develop and difficult to organize. It took awhile before we learned which areas entailed major decisions and which had only to do with organizational factors and therefore did not require a group process. It meant that people needed to accept the fact that no single group within the community had priority over another when it came to questions of human rights. This was hard to understand, because the reason for the school's existence was the education of gifted children and the adults were there to fulfill this purpose. Within this framework, however, decisions had to be made based on a philosophy of equality, for only if there is no hierarchy of justice can children ultimately be safe.

By the time of our retirement, we felt that our new structure had come of age, and we had achieved an administrative structure that expressed our philosophy. We knew, of course, that it was not perfect, and that human interaction is never smooth but is often painful and unjust, no matter how hard we try to make it otherwise.

Human reactions are influenced not only by individual personal attitudes, but also by the structure in which they function. We saw the cooperative structure of the school as a series of overlapping, concentric circles as opposed to a pyramidal hierarchy. Children and teachers formed the inner circle, with the classroom surrounding them. The classroom overlapped with special classes and other classrooms. These structures, in turn, were surrounded by the stage system and the lower and upper schools, and at the outer level by the entire school and its board. These, again, were surrounded by the community, the country, and the world. It was our hope that children who grew up in a specific community where equal human rights were valued would carry the same perception of people into the world.

There is in our society a pervasive acceptance of a hierarchy among human beings. Teachers are considered more right than children, and influential parents more right than teachers. In a structure that grows out of a deep belief in equal human rights, these unfair assumptions disappear. Children and adults develop a new sense of freedom and find it easier to express their differences openly. All of this requires very deep inner changes in the way we view and interact with one another. The education for life philosophy enables us to accomplish these goals by nurturing the resources of our inner selves and providing us with the creative skills to accomplish them.

The Gifted Child in the Nuclear Age

Proceedings of the 5th Annual Conference of *The Roeper Review* and the Academy for the Gifted and Talented, Detroit, Michigan (October, 1983).

Human relations and the dignity of students, teachers, and all others must never be forgotten. The mastery of human relations must become our top priority in education. Learning of skills and concepts in all subject areas should be in the service of human rights rather than technology or individual success. Techniques of peaceful conflict resolution, based on a framework of interdependence rather than power, should be built into the curriculum in all subjects.

We must recognize that we live in a time that has no equal. As we look back, we see that history is filled with cruelty of human beings toward each other; yet destructive forces have been paralleled by those of love and support. Over the centuries, we slowly have developed a wonderful civilization; however, we have also unleashed the most destructive powers on earth. We have unequaled expertise for healing the pain that exists on this planet and supporting a good standard of living for all, but, at the same time, we are unparalleled in our ability to destroy and harm each other. We seem to have reached the pinnacle in both positive and negative arenas. We are learning how to create life artificially and how to extend the life span, while, paradoxically, we are able to destroy our life on earth and the whole planet. What extraordinary powers we have developed! The nuclear age in which we live consists of power over the

Author's Note: While the information in this article may appear dated, as people are not as concerned today about the threat of nuclear holocaust, the danger still persists. The problem is realistically unchanged; most of all humankind is still involved in global denial of the dangers surrounding us and the fact that they are caused by our attitudes. There is also escalating world violence and terrorism, such as bombings and the release of nerve gas in public places. Therefore, it is important for all of us to become involved in protecting our children by ending violence on this planet.

life or death of every living thing on earth. Living with these amazing possibilities and opportunities, we are all trying to be in charge of this power, trying to live with it and cope with it. But again and again, we find that, instead, it has gained control over us.

How do we deal with both the monsters and the angels we have created? And how do we deal with the monsters and the angels within ourselves? How do we help the next generation to cope with these powerful forces? Our coping ability, our emotional and social attitudes, our self-control, and our self-esteem have not kept pace with our brain power and technology. We are truly lopsided.

In thinking about this subject, it has become clear to me that before we can help children deal with this crisis, we must examine our own attitudes about the reality of living at the brink of nuclear disaster. What have our attitudes been, and what are they now? I cannot help but be struck by an amazing phenomenon. We have lived in the nuclear age since World War II; it has been with us for more than a generation. Einstein, and many other scientists and futurists, have warned us about the nuclear threat, have desperately tried to impress upon us the gravity of its existence. However, until recently, the world has simply ignored it. We know that individuals have great powers of denial and often do not see what they do not want to know, but here is a case of *universal denial*, universal rejection of this threat, acting as though the reality did not exist. This is as incomprehensible as the nuclear holocaust itself. For more than a generation we have acted as though this danger did not exist. The peoples of the world seem to have united in the decision not to think about the danger of the destruction of the planet, feeling that it simply will go away. I suppose one could call it the "Emperor's New Clothes" syndrome.

In the very recent past, a growing number of us have begun to let the peril penetrate our awareness. And now we have a variety of reactions, depending on our own unique personalities, our experiences, our ages, and our personal circumstances. The vast majority continue to ignore the danger, while others feel powerless and, therefore, try to forget the situation. Some are desperate but do not know what to do, and others are concerned, but not enough to make opposing the nuclear threat a priority—to make an official commitment to it—to take a stand. Many will support nuclear disarmament privately but do not do so publicly. But millions of individuals have finally awakened to the fact that we are on the brink of losing the world.

Children, especially the gifted, have their own way of reacting. They have not learned the mechanism of denial. They are not afraid to be afraid, and therefore they look straight at the reality. They face the fact that they may not have a future. It was, after all, a child who saw that the

emperor wore no clothes. As they get older, gifted children draw practical inferences of the ever-present threat. They ask themselves, "Do I
make long-term commitments to study medicine? Will I live to be a
doctor?" Some indulge in the pleasures of the moment, such as drugs or
alcohol, rather than preparing for a future that may not exist.

Each child, of course, copes in his or her own way, but they still
differ from the adults because they know how to be afraid in a manner
with which we can hardly identify. Watch young children in their daily
lives. Note the intensity of their fears, anxieties, and hopes. They obviously feel so much more deeply than adults. We have become dulled in
our ability to feel such pain and pleasure. Over the years, I have
observed many children's reactions to being left at nursery school for the
first time by their mothers. Can we really empathize with the depth of
the child's sense of desperation and panic? Or a child feels attacked by
caterpillars. Her fear is overwhelming. Or a child has disappointed his
father. He expects something dreadful to happen. He experiences an
utmost sense of panic. In time, the child comes to realize that the terrible consequence usually does not happen. The caterpillar does not bite,
the nursery school is not so bad, the mother does return, the father's
anger gives way to a hug and love. For most children, the terrible dread
is offset by positive experiences and is eventually outgrown.

In the past, although there always have been disasters, there always
has been hope and a chance for escape. This is the picture of life por-
trayed to children by the media. Television teaches children that it is
exciting to live on the brink of disaster, and, after the next commercial,
they will be rescued. We have created a world of untruths—even for children whose lives are well protected—by trying to make them believe
that the world is really a safe place. We have done this in an effort to
make them feel better, but we also unconsciously have helped them to
acquire adult armor behind which to hide their fears.

Now the threat has become total and complete and cannot be
denied. The world can be wiped out. The dreadful, infantile anxiety is
now based on real, not imagined, danger. This real dread has enhanced
children's feelings of powerlessness and their feelings that the adults do
not care enough about them to protect them—that we cannot or will not
try to make this a safe world. They feel that we do not identify with their
fears. One way they try to counteract such dread is to fantasize having
power and getting revenge; they dream of dropping the bomb, of being
the destroyers. Many teachers have told me about children who play
atomic war. This is their attempt to gain some type of mastery over the
situation, because otherwise it would be unbearable. These children,
average and gifted alike, see their chances for a future realistically. The
threat of global annihilation is a fact of life for them. Each will deal with

this fact differently. Some are angry, some feel hopeless, many cannot decide about careers, and younger children have nightmares and dreams. Mostly, they feel abandoned and unprotected by adults and by society, and this also is a reality. It is reality because we leave them alone to face this threat while we hide our heads in the sand.

When children are born we give them a promise—a promise to protect them and support them and make the world a safe place for them until they are able to become secure adults who can take over and do the same for the next generation. I do not believe that humankind has ever fulfilled this promise to its children. Adults have always used children for their own purposes, to fulfill their own needs. Society has sent our young to fight our wars for us. This, I think, is a symbol of how we have used our children. Have children ever been safe? My answer is yes and no.

Many children have been give much love, support, understanding, and protection, but others have been neglected, abandoned, or abused by adults who have shown no concern for their needs. Now we are at the point where the difference between using them and protecting them is a matter of life and death. Out of this decision grows our reaction to our present unprecedented life situation.

Parents and educators are by nature advocates of the future; it is safe to assume that all of us want our children to have not only a future, but a happy, healthy, and safe one. We are also, by nature, optimists. We could not do our work, we could not have children, if we did not believe in the future, and this is realistic also. As long as we are still here, there is hope. And I believe that opportunity now exists to change the direction in which we are going. The responsibility to make sure there is a future rests with every one of us.

What, then, is our task? In my mind, this task involves many aspects. First, we must clarify our own attitudes and beliefs. Do we believe in peace? Do we want to preserve the world? Do we believe that we are in danger of exterminating ourselves? Do we think it is up to us to do something about this danger? Do we think it is up to us to protect our children? Do we think that we have the personal power to do this? Do we think that we can bring about change? Do we think that changing the world situation must become a priority in daily life? Do we think that nuclear war is both impossible to win and immoral even to prepare for? Do we think that a limited nuclear war is immoral? Do we believe that the world is interdependent? Do we believe that there never can be winners or losers in a war? Do we believe that the Russian child and the Lebanese child have as much right to live as our child does? Do we believe in our personal and combined strength? My personal answer, of course, is yes to all of these questions, and, because of this, I feel there are many realistic inferences to be drawn by all of those who join me in these convictions. We must come out from behind our armor, which the child has not yet developed. We might need to learn fear from our children in order to understand them and to help them. We must learn to face reality rather than teach the child to cover it up. In order to help the child, we need to face ourselves. Today, Roosevelt's famous words, "We have nothing to fear but fear itself," must be interpreted differently. We have to fear the fear which cannot face itself and therefore ignores itself. *Our greatest danger is our lack of fear.*

We need to realize that our concern with survival must become a priority, a part of our daily consciousness. It will not help to give our lives over to panic; instead, we need to keep our survival in mind as we keep in mind that we and our children need to be taken care of daily and always. We take for granted that food and shelter are our first priorities. The question of total survival is just as important, even though less visible; it is a daily moral priority.

Once we have faced this, how do we help our children? First, we must accept, and empathize with, the reality of their fears and the reality of the object of their fears. In the past, when children were afraid of fire, we could soothe them and make them feel secure. It was usually not a realistic fear. Now, however, the world might catch on fire at any moment, and protecting our children from it must come before anything else. I think we need to show our empathy and recognition of reality by telling children that we understand their dread, we feel it just as strongly as they do, and we will keep our promise to them to protect them to the best of our ability by concentrating on keeping the house—their world—from burning.

How do we prove this to them? How do we do this? Many children would like their parents and teachers to become activists. But they usually see little interest on the part of adults in their lives in getting involved in saving the world; therefore, many children feel that it has become up to them to keep themselves safe, and that makes them feel deserted. We must give them back their childhoods by letting them know that we feel positive about our own strength, that we think we can do it together with all the others who care.

I am aware that this is a very difficult task. Educators and parents are often afraid to act; they are afraid of offending neighbors or of losing political support or antagonizing some person or organization. This is when children—particularly gifted children—feel most unprotected, because they are aware that their parents and teachers are pursuing the wrong priorities. They see that their parents dare not take risks in daily matters, and that this may lead to risking their children's lives and futures. They realize that the sum of such daily risks may save them and the world.

The avenues available at this point are too numerous to enumerate here, but there are many ways in which you can take a stand. To me, one of the important ones is to make sure that the school your child goes to has taken an official stand for global nuclear disarmament. This is also the best psychological protection you can give your children. They will realize they are growing up in an environment which cares for them and tries to preserve their future. You can be active through your church or synagogue, you can take a stand with your employers, you can work for candidates, write your congressperson, join peace organizations. Much of this may entail risks of disapproval and worse. Let your children know about your involvement and participate in your activities, but also let them know that you see it as your responsibility. This way, you will be doing two things simultaneously: political action for the world, and personal, psychological action for yourself and your family. You will make a political impact, and you will show your child you care. This is what children want from their parents. Many children have told me this, and many adults have told me that they have heard the same from other children. This is political action for survival.

This brings up a new problem. It asks that you look at roles and institutional structures in a different manner than is usually done. Traditionally, educators prepare for the future, and governments insure the existence of the future for the individual. If you look at history, you see that this division of labor has never worked very well. Now it does not seem to be working at all, because the government's respect for the individual seems to have sunk to an all-time low. The concept of "limited nuclear warfare" expresses the greatest disrespect for the individual. It makes the individual a number, a stepping-stone—nonexistent in terms of his or her personal rights. Today, therefore, the task of the educator, and parent, changes to include both the preparation for the future and its preservation. It is my opinion that educators and parents who are committed to the future must become activists, must do all they can to minimize the threat of nuclear war in order to be true to their own commitment to life and children.

You might object that education should not be political. My answer to this objection is two-fold: First, we have reached a point where we cannot separate education from politics, for politics has become concerned with survival. And second, taking an active stand for global nuclear disarmament is, in my opinion, one of the most educational activities we can undertake. It helps us preserve the only framework in which children can be free to grow and learn, by providing the protective measures necessary for the feeling of safety. Many people who are committed to peace and against nuclear warfare do not take this particular step. They believe that it is their task to provide children with knowledge of the nuclear age, and help them cope with it in an educational manner through appropriate curriculum. I also believe this is important, but I think it is unrealistic to limit our activities to just this approach. We must learn to really change the status quo, not spend our energies teaching the children to cope with it.

When polio was a dangerous illness, we did not create a curriculum to help children learn to live with polio. Instead, medical research eradicated it. In the same manner, eradication of nuclear danger is our task, not accepting it as a fact of life and teaching our children to live with it. Therefore, this is the strongest point I would like to make today: *If we are true educators and parents, and if we love our children, we must spare no effort to actively stand up for global nuclear disarmament.* This is the short-range plan that I think we must commit ourselves to.

I think there is also deep and long-range thinking yet to be done. We need to ask the questions, "Why do we find ourselves in the predicament we are in now? What has brought us to this point? How did we get where we are? What are the human forces that create conflict?" Our present state of affairs must be seen as a symptom of our approach to life. We must recognize the fact that innate aggression exists in each human being. We cannot deny this fact or wish it away. We cannot tell the child not to be angry and then expect the anger simply to go away. Human aggression is a fact of life, also. It exists in both students and teachers. It must be recognized as a reality and dealt with realistically—not suppressed, but expressed and sublimated in a socially acceptable manner. This, then, leads us to the type of human interaction necessary in educational institutions, classrooms, and in the family. In order to help us handle our society better, in order to solve its problems by better means, we need to create, for children and adults, an atmosphere where individuals feel enough confidence and support to find channels of acceptable communication for expressing their feelings, both negative and positive.

Human relations and the dignity of students, teachers, and all others must never be forgotten. The mastery of human relations must become our top priority in education. Learning of skills and concepts in all subject areas should be in the service of human rights rather than technology or individual success. Techniques of peaceful conflict resolution, based on a framework of interdependence rather than power, should be built into the curriculum in all subjects. One of the most destructive attitudes in education is the idea of teaching subjects devoid of the moral consequences they entail. It is especially important for gifted students to be taught the complexity of decision-making based on conservation of human rights, as well as taught to understand the many sides of each question. They have the advanced awareness and abstract reasoning needed to deal with this level of complexity. All curriculum—particularly in science and social studies—should be looked at from a global perspective, from the point of view of human rights. What advantages and disadvantages can this new knowledge bring? What is its positive and negative potential?

We must develop real empathy—we much teach the complex consequences of our actions. History and politics should be taught in terms of circles of reactions and interdependence, rather than in a linear cause-and-effect manner. The school community is a world in miniature and can be used for these purposes. There are always many causes and many effects, and they all depend on each other. Even with a young child we can show the circle of effects of his or her actions. We can teach the connection. We can teach empathy if we have it ourselves.

We have learned the techniques of competition, but humans are also cooperative by nature, and we have not developed the skills of cooperation enough. We need to learn and teach techniques of cooperation and conflict resolution, and we need to know and believe that this can be done and that it can be applied to the whole world. It is because we doubt that this can work in the real world that we neglect to apply cooperative principles in our institutions.

The attitude of the institution and the behavior of the adults as role models are the hidden curriculum of an educational institution. These must also be humanistic and champion human rights. Children react more to the hidden curriculum than to the conscious one. They will sense if the teacher is more concerned with impressing the principal than with meeting the needs of the students. We need humanistic institutions, institutions run by justice, not power, in order to raise children who understand the skills of cooperation.

You may think these suggestions are far-fetched from the danger of living in a nuclear age and from doing something about it. I think *stress on cooperative human relations is the real curriculum of peace,* the real crux of the problem. I know that I have only touched upon it very superficially, for it is in reality the most complex issue in the world.

I am only trying to raise our consciousness in terms of priorities for the framework in which modern education should take place. I think our lack of knowledge about cooperation, interdependence, and mutual empathy are the reasons we have come to the brink of annihilation. I believe, therefore, that our task is threefold:

1. to raise children who are not angry and consequently can be rational in their thinking;

2. to raise children who learn to use their skills, knowledge, and intelligence to better the fate of the world rather than cope with the existing status quo; and

3. to raise children who view themselves as their brother's keepers.

In order to accomplish this, we need to develop these attitudes, emotions, and actions in ourselves so we can be models, protectors, and activists. Only then can we make our children feel respected, loved, and protected, so that they may be free to grow without an armor of denial, and use their full potential for themselves and all humanity. Politics are truly made in the cradle.

We must educate children about nuclear dangers at the appropriate age, but not make them feel responsible. We must deal with their fears realistically, but protect them with our own belief in our responsibility to bring about change in this situation. We must accept the fact that life is no longer business as usual. Survival must be our top priority. Commitment to making survival the priority brings with it an extremely positive experience. You will find that you are not alone. You will become a member of a world community of caring, morally mature individuals. This community is banding together more and more all over the world with the common goal of creating real peace and a future for our children.

What I Have Learned
from Gifted Children

Speech delivered at the California Association for Gifted Conference in Oakland, California (February, 1986).

Gifted children have taught me about themselves, who they are, how they feel, what is important to them, how they differ from other children, how they are like other children, how they differ from one another, and what they have in common.

Gifted children have given me many moments of pleasure and stimulation. I have spent many years living with gifted children, their parents, and their teachers. I have worked and played with gifted children, talked with them, and listened to them and to their parents. I have had disagreements with them and some hard times. Most of all, I have been surprised by much that I have observed, and I have learned a great deal from them.

1. Gifted children have taught me about themselves, who they are, how they feel, what is important to them, how they differ from other children, how they are like other children, how they differ from one another, and what they have in common.

2. I have learned about their specific needs for a learning environment, about what gifted children need to learn, how they need to learn it, what is missing for them in traditional educational institutions, and, most important, what is a good learning environment for all children, along with what is missing for all children in the traditional learning environment.

3. I have learned about the role of adults, especially parents and teachers, in the world of the gifted, how it differs from the role adults play for all children, and how it is alike. I have also learned how adults

see themselves in relation to the gifted as well as to all children, and in turn the impact this has on the gifted and others.

4. I have seen the world through the eyes of the gifted, who usually have a global point of view, the capacity and tendency to see the whole rather than the parts, to see not sequentially but complexly, who often have a deep sense of justice, who have a tendency to see the connections. They have given support to my view that education cannot exist in isolation but must relate to a philosophy and the realities of life. I probably cannot say that all of my thoughts and ideas originate with the gifted, but much of my philosophy has been triggered by my work with them.

When children are born anywhere in the world—I think this applies even to the animal child—they enter the world with silent expectations for food, shelter, love, support, protection, and the opportunity to grow to their fullest capacity. They also expect that they will be received into a livable world. These are the silent expectations of the children of the world, and these are the promises they are given by parents and teachers. How are these expectations and promises fulfilled? I think I have found some answers to this question in my work with the gifted, answers for gifted children and for all children. I will use some practical examples to help me make my points.

CASE HISTORY I

The mother of an eight-year-old boy came to see me. She was desperate; she simply could not get along with him. He had been identified as gifted, with an IQ of 160. But every day the mother had to talk to his teacher because the boy was not doing his homework. He did not pay attention; he daydreamed most of the time. And he had few, if any, friends. Though he had been reading since he was four, he had not been placed in the first reading group because he neglected to finish his reading assignments. However, at home he read technical and scientific books or *National Geographic* endlessly. His conversation, his remarks, his interests often amazed his parents.

The parents had no problems with his two younger sisters, but the boy, their eldest child, was much more work than the two little ones together. He was jealous of his little sisters and often mistreated them. He would not do what his parents asked of him. He was often depressed, fought with them, would never clean up his room, and so on. At times the mother and son had conversations which made her understand him a little better, but the father was getting more and more disenchanted

and wanted to send the boy to military school. This had also created conflict between the parents. The mother wanted everybody to be happy,
but did not know how to accomplish this. The boy often said, "I'd like to
kill myself." From all of this, it was hard not to conclude that this was a
problem child, or at least a child with problems. I looked forward to the
interview with the child, but I did not know what to expect.

From the first moment, I was surprised. I felt that I was confronted
with a unique personality. I could talk to the boy as I could with an adult.
His vocabulary was outstanding and rich, enabling him to describe his
present situation at home and school in vivid terms. He developed an
immediate confidence in me and knew the purpose of our interview.
The first thing he talked about was his feelings of guilt. "I'm a misfit," he
said. "I create trouble for my teachers and my family. I wish I could be
like my sister; she makes good grades, and the teachers and my parents
love her. My biggest problem is my daydreaming. I simply can't help it."
And he told me about his dreams of a world without war, his fear of
nuclear weapons, and how and why solar energy is so much better than
other forms of energy. He told me about what we have done to the environment and how the "white man's" relationship to nature is different
from that of Native Americans. He supported all this with an amazing
amount of facts and concepts. He liked to talk about these things to a girl
he knew, but he could not talk to her at school "because whoever heard
of an eight-year-old boy liking girls? That shows you how strange I am.
My dad thinks that's strange, too. And he doesn't know why I don't have
friends. I like sports, but somehow other kids don't seem to like me." He
loved animals, but was allergic to them and was not allowed to have any
pets. He also said, "Why am I so bored at school? I learned more on the
train trip through the country than I ever did at school."

I cannot stress enough that this was not a problem child. But there
was a problem: the interaction between him and his school, home, and
neighborhood environments. Why? He did not meet their expectations;
he was different. School curricula, home routines, parental hopes and
goals, and the means of achieving them are based on the way most
people are and on the way they generally see the world. He did not fit
any of their criteria. This, then, created anger and disappointment in the
adults, as well as fear of personal failure and guilt. All these feelings also
existed in the boy and influenced his emotional development, his academic growth, and his self-image. Because he naturally accepted the
standards of his environment rather than his own and failed by those
standards, he did not feel recognized or valued for the person he really
was and therefore did not value himself. He tried to live up to others'
expectations. "I am teaching myself not to daydream," he said. "I asked
my teacher to move my desk away from the window into a corner,

where nothing would start me dreaming and where I would not wonder about the distant land the bird is flying to or watch the clouds to see when they would be filled with enough moisture to burst." Then he added, "I try to make my teachers understand me and my mother love me as much as she loves my sisters." He saw himself as a problem, his special abilities as liabilities rather than as assets.

What created this problem of interaction? His giftedness actually worked against him. His environment could not help but know that he was a gifted child. It was obvious. His vocabulary was extremely sophisticated, as was his knowledge of science and the environment. His IQ was a known. No one else in the class had tested as high as he had. His teachers felt that he should have been the best student in the class, but that he was just lazy. He *could* have been the best student in the class. The question is, why *wasn't* he?

I believe the answer is that the areas in which he was vitally interested were given low priority in the eyes of his teachers. His interests lay in the environment, science, art, geography, and social studies. These were on his mind all the time. He was thirsting for information about these things, but they were not part of the curriculum, so he felt frustrated. He knew a great deal about these subjects, and anyone who listened to him would learn something, would be stimulated to learn more, and would be impressed with his knowledge. Had these areas been given priority in his school's curriculum, he would have had the opportunity to share his knowledge and ideas and receive positive feedback. Instead, he experienced only negative feedback. In a different learning environment, he would have been able to learn more about the world. His goal was to master the world, to understand it and make it his own. He was not motivated by outward success. He would have liked to receive good marks to please his teachers, but not for himself. What he really needed from his environment was support, approval, and protection from the wrong expectations. He needed people—adults and children—who shared his interests. He needed to be given the opportunity to grow and learn in his own way.

How did this child appear from his teacher's point of view? She had a specific curriculum to teach and specific learning objectives to achieve. This was required of her. The structure, the goals, the methods of achieving them, the expectations of the children—all had become the norm—unquestioned over the years. The teacher felt threatened in her ability to achieve these goals as well as threatened by the child's intelligence. She honestly tried to help, but she was unable to understand or change. There was a true communication gap between them. This frustrated her and made her feel both guilty and angry. And so the frequent conferences with the mother.

The father had high hopes for his son, but found that his son was different from all the neighbors' children. That wounded his pride and made him angry and anxious. What was to be done? In counseling this family, I was able to make a difference. I was able to help the parents to see that they had a child of whom they could be proud, not ashamed. I was able to help the child understand that he was not guilty, that he could be proud of himself; that opened up communication between him and his parents. Most of all, I was able to convince the parents that it was necessary for the child to be transferred to a school with a more individualized structure and teachers who did not feel threatened. He needed a school where there were other children who were gifted and with whom he could really communicate. He needed an environment that paid attention to the emotions and the development of the self. He needed acceptance, empathy, and respect as a unique human being. Once it was recognized that he was not "a problem," but rather the interaction with the environment was the problem, he was transferred to a new school. The school was not one specifically for the gifted, but the philosophy of the school was to look at each child as an individual, so it was more responsive to his abilities. At this point, our consultation ended.

CASE HISTORY II

The second case history I would like to describe concerns a little girl who was brought to me at the age of five. Her mother told me that she was going to a very small nursery school and that it was impossible for any of her teachers to handle her. In fact, she disrupted the whole program. The teachers, especially the director, felt threatened by her. The child acted superior to them and would not listen to anything they said to her. If anybody made a demand on her, she would become physically aggressive, destroy material, and so on. This was terribly upsetting to her teachers. The mother happened to work in the same nursery school, and it was always very difficult for her to pick up the pieces after these incidents.

At home, there was an older brother who was ill and who was also gifted, but not quite as gifted as his younger sister. The little girl felt that she was in charge of the household. In talking to the mother, it became clear that she was in awe of her daughter and felt that everything should be done to support her gifts. The little girl was extremely gifted: She had taught herself to read and was able to do difficult math problems. The mother came from a family where there were five children and every one of them, as well as their mother, was gifted. Emphasis was put on giftedness, and there was a great deal of competition among her and her siblings. This mother felt that she herself was the least gifted of them all.

The mother said that her daughter would not accept any authority, and had once attacked a baby-sitter with a knife when the sitter told her to go to bed. When the child first came to see me, she walked in with her back sort of bent, and she looked very sad and depressed. I said, "You look as if you're carrying the burdens of the world on your back." And she said, "I am. Nothing goes right at home if I don't take care of it. I'm responsible for everything. And I also have ESP. The other day I knew we were going to see a car accident, and a few minutes later, we saw one on the street." She felt omnipotent. She accepted me because she knew I had run a school for gifted children and I knew something about the gifted. I saw her once a week for about a year. She expressed her feelings and spoke openly to me. We played games and talked. Slowly, I got it across to her that it was safe to be a child and that her parents were going to take care of her, that she did not need to take care of them. At the same time, I needed to work with the parents and make it clear to them that they were in charge, that she was really a very anxious little girl who did not feel that she should have the responsibility for everything that went on in her family.

After seeing me for a year, she entered a public school and had a better year, but still not a very good one. She was put a year ahead of her age group, but her teacher did not want to recognize the fact that she was gifted. Instead, the teacher noticed only the gaps in her knowledge of math and other subjects. The teacher kept letting her know that she was not the outstanding person that everybody else had made her out to be. This only gave her negative feedback; it did not help her. It was obvious that she was the best student in the class and was a truly gifted child, but she did not get any positive support for this. However, with my constant support things seemed to improve, at least to the extent that she was able to go to school without proving her superiority by engaging in destructive behavior. The bickering and aggression and guilt toward her older brother diminished a great deal.

The following year, the mother insisted that the child be put in a class that was two years advanced. At the age of seven, the girl was placed in a combination fourth/fifth-grade class. She had a teacher who was supposed to be someone who understood gifted children. Even at that level, the child was doing better than most of the other children. But still, this teacher seemed to carry the same kind of resentment that the child had experienced before. The teacher told the other students that the girl was just a "baby," that they should take care of her, look after her, not be upset if she did not have as long an attention span as they did, and so on. So she was both the highest and the lowest in the group. The children began to tease her unmercifully. At that point, the parents talked to me and I talked to the teacher, who said to me that if the girl was gifted, she must learn to stand on her own feet and be able to defend herself against that group of children. I had tried to let the child know that she was a child and that adults did take care of her, that she would not have to take care of her own problems. She came to me and said, "You didn't tell me the truth. You've really been lying to me, because adults do *not* take care of me. I have to fight and take care of myself when all these children who are two years older than I am turn against me. Now I can't even trust you anymore." It took me a long time to help her get over this. In fact, the only way I could finally help her was to convince her parents to take her out of that school. They did, and sent her to our school in Michigan. The interesting thing was that the problems quickly came to a halt after that. She was placed in a non-graded group where there were other children her age. She found others who performed at the same level as she did and who supported her. The acting-out behavior and the depression disappeared within two weeks. It was amazing for all of us to observe.

Then her father was transferred to a different state where she had to enroll in the neighborhood school. I began receiving letters from her and her mother saying that the problems had begun all over again. I cite this example to point out, again, that it only *looked* as though the child had severe problems, when the reality was that the environment could not live up to her particular needs, mostly her need for emotional support.

Why can't gifted children fit into traditional learning environments? Although there are many reasons for this, I can enumerate only a few of them here. There is a general misunderstanding about the specific characteristics, developmental phases, and self-image of the gifted child. Many gifted children are not skill learners; they are concept learners. They do not necessarily excel in skill areas. Yet it is skills that are expected of them—by parents and teachers—and it becomes a puzzle to adults that their children cannot fulfill these expectations when they are considered to be gifted.

Also, adults are disappointed when gifted children are, for example, not the best readers in their class. In reality, reading is not necessarily a sign of giftedness. There are many gifted children who are not early or outstanding readers. There are also children who are not gifted but who are nonetheless excellent readers. Once gifted children become readers, they love books and become deeply engrossed in them, for they realize that books are a great resource for concept learning, information, and enjoyment. However, they consider reading as their own property; they often have interests that are not covered by, for instance, the classics or other reading materials prescribed by adults. They often do not like being quizzed about their ability to comprehend. They want to own their reading experience. Gifted children need open, individualized education and opportunities to develop their own interests, yet enough traditional education to build a bridge between the two. All children need emotional support and individual recognition. This is especially true for gifted children.

Another misconception about gifted children is the expectation that their emotional development will take care of itself and that, because they are gifted, it is their intellects that need to be developed. The reality is that these children, because of their giftedness, often have different emotional reactions and different feelings of self than do some other children. Their selves and self-images, in fact, are often small and immature and need help along the developmental road. This is often very difficult for adults to understand. In the regular school curriculum, there is really no space for or emphasis on the growth of the self and the emotions. There is no word for the *unique self* in conventional education. Gifted children need acceptance of their uniqueness and their differences, and they need help in bridging the gap that exists between them and other children. They also need an adult who understands them. They need someone who can be a model for them, who is like them, and who can show that one can grow up and master the world.

There exists a mutual disappointment, actually. Gifted children often do not fulfill the expectations of adults and vice versa. There are times when the children are seen as antagonists, and they are aware that this is the way they are seen, as in cases when adults are threatened by them. There are also situations in which adults feel that their children give them a second chance. If they have not succeeded in life as much as they had hoped to, they see in their children—be it children in their classroom or their own children—as another opportunity to prove themselves. Gifted children realize this, and they fear that they have to succeed in order to fulfill the needs of the adults. It is for this reason that many gifted children feel that their successes belong to their parents and that their failures belong to themselves.

Gifted children have a need to make sense of the world. They have a need to see the connections. They have a great sense of justice. For these reasons, they look for a philosophy of education during their school years. They want to know why they are learning what they have to learn. They want to know the connection between what they are learning and the state of the world. So they look for a philosophy of education and a philosophy of life. They have a tendency to ponder the reasons for the existence of the universe, the existence of our own planet, the existence of the human race, and, most of all, the purpose of their own existence. Even young gifted children—three, four, or five years old—often wonder about life and death. They often have an acute fear of death and many other concerns. They worry about the future—their own and that of the world.

Schools rarely take time to help children explore such questions. Neither do many parents. Most schools do not build their curriculum on a philosophy of education. They are usually limited in the scope of their objectives and are therefore isolated from life. Often they are reduced to preparing their students for the next grade level or teacher. A kindergarten teacher prepares her students for first-grade teachers so they will not think her a bad teacher. Elementary education prepares for high school, high school for college, and college for career. Preparation for life, or the thought that life is being lived while we are preparing, often falls by the wayside. Yet the gifted need to see the connection between life and their studies. All children need this, but gifted children experience this need more intensely.

Every child is unique, and each has a desire to master the world, to make it his or her own, and to be respected and supported by it. Everybody is restricted by the arbitrary goals of society, which may or may not fit the needs and abilities of the individual. Education tends to function as if all children are the same, learn in the same manner, and have the same interests and abilities. It is as though every six-year-old wore the same size, was built in the same manner, and looked good in the same clothes. In truth, our educational systems fit few children, gifted or not.

Most children accept the status quo, however. They try to fit into it and manage quite well in the areas in which they are expected to function. Other areas are rather hit-or-miss but go unnoticed. Gifted children are often aware of their own needs, and aware of the narrowness and inflexibility of the educational system. Because they are questioners and critical thinkers, they find such an education lacking. Educators have drawn the conclusion that the traditional content and process of education are inappropriate for gifted children and have begun to plan separate programs for them. It is my sincere belief that the principles that guide education for the gifted represent good education for all. If we think that only the gifted need a different education, we are wrong. This is one of the things I have learned from gifted children: What they need in education applies to all children. Gifted children simply make these needs more evident.

Education should be individualized in purpose and expectation. It should be cooperative, not competitive, in structure. This does not mean isolation, for children need the stimulation of others and the feeling of belonging to the group. Education should be a participatory process—

active, doing, not being done to, based on the inquiry method. It should include concept learning as well as skill learning; it should include many opportunities for creativity and for joy, such as art, music, nature studies, dance, and drama. These should have equal status with reading and math. Social studies, science, and other challenging subjects should be included early on in the curriculum. All these build on natural motivation and should be available from the start.

Education should also deal with ethical questions. It should be focused on the emotional, moral, and ethical development of the student rather than on preparation for success in the work world. It should be centered on the development of the self, assisting the student through the normal developmental phases. This developmental process is often hindered by the expectations of adults. Success in traditional terms is likely to be a natural byproduct of an education focused on the individual needs of the child. Educators must forget about preparing children for the next step; rather, the next step should adapt to the child. Teachers need to understand themselves so that they can answer honestly, "Are we fulfilling our own needs rather than the child's?" They should take their position as role models as seriously as they do their roles as teachers. In order to do that, they themselves need to feel nurtured and supported and in charge of their own destinies. It is my belief that educators need to think about who they are rather than what they can do. Only then can they help children to grow up to be who they really are.

The problems of the gifted are almost always in an area of growth of the self. We can help by respecting their uniqueness, supporting their special interests, empathizing with their deep feelings, building bridges between themselves and others, protecting them from hostility, understanding the phases of development, and learning about the experience of giftedness. Gifted children realize that the learning community does not fulfill their needs, and they often react to this with feelings of confusion, bewilderment, depression, and powerlessness.

Gifted children are like other children in most respects. They need acceptance, guidance, support, respect, love, protection, and the opportunity to grow without artificial distortions of their innate needs. This is true for all children. Children need to live in a world that is relevant. They need to grow in an educational environment that prepares them to make sense of the real world and gives them the tools to change it. The difference is that gifted children know this and can articulate it, while others just accept it. However, despite their awareness, the gifted are influenced by the artificial values of the educational system nonetheless. I have learned from them that education has become a one-sided instrument. It relates to academic learning, but does not stress the development and the growth of the self. Yet it is this inner self, the unique self of each human being, that is the central point of their lives. How children cope with life will depend on the strength of their self, whether they are gifted or not.

Most of all, I have learned from gifted children that we cannot separate education from life or from events that affect our planet. Gifted children, more than others, question and ponder what the world is like and what they and we adults can do to make it better. The questions I hear most from gifted children are, "Why don't adults do anything about the state of the world? Why are we allowing the environment to be destroyed? Why are we allowing nuclear power to threaten our universe?" Why *don't* we adults do anything? The average child deplores the terrible tragedy that happened to the space shuttle *Challenger* and the people in it, but gifted children question our reliance on technology, wonder why it happened, and wonder whether the tragedy could have been prevented.

One of the most important things I have learned from gifted children is that they ask questions we would rather not hear. They make us uncomfortable. They question our complacency and why we are not actively involved in saving the world. I consider this to be part of the curriculum. I feel that concerns about life on earth should be expressed and discussed at every educational level so that children can relate to them. There should be opportunities for children to learn methods of conflict resolution, to have and express a global understanding of the peoples and the nature of the world. After all, they do worry about it. They want to feel that we who are now adults are doing all that we can to protect them. This is the message that gifted children have given me. It is an important one to which I earnestly hope all of us will listen.

Parenting the Gifted

The main body of this article was delivered at a parent meeting at Hillview Crest School, Union City Public Schools, Union City, California (January, 1986). The ten points at the end of the article come from a speech delivered at Greenfield Community College, Greenfield, Massachusetts (Spring, 1986).

Gifted children are not better or faster than others, nor do they necessarily excel in the usually considered areas. They are basically different from other children. Very often, they are not skill learners; they are concept learners instead, so that in elementary school their giftedness may actually work against them. They have that special awareness. They are concerned with the complexities of the world. There are many factors, such as personal concerns, anxiety, or perfectionism, that might keep a gifted child from mastering school subjects, but we must be aware that what they do learn is often unique.

It is a strange realization to find out that one's child is gifted. Pride and worry mingle with feelings of apprehension. "Will I be able to live up to this challenge?" "How can I give to my child the opportunities appropriate to his or her potential?" These questions often become uppermost in parents' minds. Here is an example. A young child's head got caught in a revolving door. His parents had just found out that he was extremely gifted. His mother told me later that she found herself worrying about his valuable brain rather than the possibility that he might be injured! When parents know that their child is gifted, they become bewildered; they do not know what to expect. They do not know how much responsibility and how much freedom to give the child. Should they treat him or her like an adult or like a child? Even before their child's giftedness is confirmed, parents observe differences in the child's reactions and behavior. They realize that their child acts and reacts differently from other children. They find that their child does not fit the norm, and this realization is puzzling and stressful.

Gifted children have a tendency to surprise us with their advanced abilities, their knowledge, their ability to generalize, their sensitivity, their astute observations, their mature logic, their insights, their unusual interests, their incredible memories, and so forth. On the other hand, they often appear infantile, they may be argumentative, and they have a tendency to be loners. Many seem to be unable to fit into a regular classroom. There are gifted children who can read at age two; there are other gifted children who do not begin to read until age eight. I remember a little five-year-old boy who could do algebra at the age of two; he spoke French fluently; he could also play the piano. But at the age of five he was still not toilet-trained. These are the kinds of unexpected experiences that parents are often exposed to with gifted children. Of course, one uses the extreme to make a point, and not every gifted child exhibits such extreme behavior.

What is a parent to do? What is he or she to think? What is a parent to feel? Every situation is different, so whatever I say may or may not be meaningful to each of you. There are, however, a few guidelines that might be helpful to all of you. First, it is important to acknowledge that raising gifted children is both a wonderful, unique experience and also a great challenge. This experience begins at birth, because gifted children are different from the day they are born; they don't become different all of a sudden. Newborn babies have an awareness, a liveliness, and, sometimes, a nervousness that is quite apparent. Second, they are different from others in some very fundamental ways, and they are like others in some fundamental ways. They are global thinkers at an early age. They see the whole before they see the parts. There is an excitement and maturity about them, and at the same time, they will cry for their mothers like any young child might. Third, we cannot have the same expectations of them that we apply to other children. In fact, we must forget about the usual expectations. We must expect the unexpected and accept this as the reality for these particular children. This often means that they will not live up to our neighbors' standards, because the gifted child will do things that seem unusual to our neighbors, and unusual to us as well, both in the positive and negative sense. A child of five may sit in a doorway alternately reading a love story and a book about how to build intricate buildings. In addition, we need to remember that no matter how overwhelmed we might be with the fact that we have a gifted child, we have needs, too; we must not forget ourselves and our own needs, and we must also realize that these needs are separate from those of the child.

Besides the real difficulties of raising gifted children, there are misconceptions about them which are often confusing for parents. Once we realize that they are gifted, we sometimes feel that they should be ahead of others their age academically—better than anybody else. I remember when we ran our school in Michigan that many parents expected their children to score at least two years ahead of others on standardized tests. And if the scores did not meet their expectations, they felt that something was wrong and that somebody was to be blamed for it—the child, the teacher, or themselves. It is very important to realize that this is not the case. Gifted children are not better or faster than others, nor do they necessarily excel in the usually considered areas. They are basically *different* from other children. Very often, they are not skill learners; they are concept learners instead, so that in elementary school their giftedness may actually work against them. They have that special awareness. They are concerned with the complexities of the world. There are many factors, such as personal concerns, anxiety, or perfectionism, that might keep a gifted child from mastering school subjects, but we must be aware that what they *do* learn is often unique. Their interests may be very specialized. The regular curriculum is not geared to the minds of the gifted, and yet they are expected to perform as if it were.

These misconceptions can lead to some real tragedies, because children who are expected to excel in areas in which they are either uninterested or unable to excel are not recognized as gifted. Recently, I saw a little girl who seemed to be an average learner except that her parents and teacher felt that there was something unusual about her. Her understanding of concepts, her language ability, her whole approach to life seemed so different, so much more logical, so much more advanced in understanding than other children. And yet her academic work did not show any of this, and resulted in a refusal by her school to allow the girl to be tested for the gifted and talented program. When an intelligence test was finally administered, she was found to have an IQ of 180. She was interested in chemistry and nature studies and in many other things that children her age are not usually knowledgeable about.

Traditionally, the whole emphasis in the gifted child movement has been on helping children grow academically and, to some degree, in the development of their creative abilities. To me, this represents another misconception—that gifted children crave academic success. While opportunities for intellectual, academic, and conceptual development are certainly an enormous need for gifted children, this need does not grow out of their desire for success; it comes from the emotional necessity to master and understand their environment. Therefore, I believe that the first priority in meeting the needs of gifted children is emotional support from the adults in their environment.

It might come as a surprise to you that gifted children very often have low self-images. There are several reasons for this. They have a tendency to be perfectionists, and, as such, fail to live up to the expectations that they set for themselves. They also feel that they do not live up to the expectations of their environment. In my experience, many parents see their gifted children as an extension of themselves. Their children are strongly aware of this and feel that they are not living up to their parents' expectations of them. In these cases, they also feel that their successes belong to their parents, while their failures belong to them. Even when gifted children have parental support, they often feel somewhat out of place with peers, school, and the world around them. Because gifted children are in the minority, it is easy for them to feel that others are the norm and they are abnormal. For instance, one six-year-old boy told me that he always felt as though he were a Martian. He felt that he did not belong on this planet; he was only a guest on this earth. Gifted children see the complexities of the world but feel powerless to contend with their advanced awareness. They often feel at a loss as to how to cope with their life situations.

I knew a 15-year-old boy who received bad marks all the time because he did not do his homework, he did not pay attention in class, and so on. When I talked to him, he said that there was nothing in the world that he would rather do than be one of the group and to be successful, but he was driven to write a symphony. He kept hearing the notes in his mind all the time, and, as much as he tried, he simply could not concentrate on what was expected of him. In cases like this, parents need to be very supportive. It is important to realize that what the child is doing is basically positive, even if it differs from the expected.

Parents need to be advocates for their gifted children, while, at the same time, building bridges so that the children will also learn the things that are necessary for them to live with others. Because of their special interests, strong desires and opinions, and enormous energy that may be combined with less need for sleep, it is often difficult for parents to raise these children. It takes a great deal of energy and concentration to raise a gifted child. It is important that parents be aware of this and not feel that they are failing. It is difficult, also, to allow the child to fulfill his or her own destiny, especially if it differs from what is expected by other people. I remember many students who were accepted in the best Eastern colleges upon graduation from our school, but who chose either not to go to college at all for awhile or to go to some unknown little college that happened to offer the particular specialization in which they were interested.

Such decisions may disappoint parents unless they can really accept that their child must go where he or she needs to go.

It is also very important that we make sure that there is a normal, well-defined parent-child relationship, in which the parent is the adult and the child is the child. If not, a gifted child inadvertently can become the head of the family, with his opinion always consulted—especially in a single-parent family. If parents are in awe of their child's giftedness and knowledge, he can suddenly become the leader in the family. And that, of course, frightens him, because he knows he is not really capable of doing that. Such children feel that they are solely responsible for whatever happens in the family. I remember a little girl of five who came to my office to talk with me. She walked in with her shoulders bent, sort of shuffling in, and I said to her, "You look as if you're carrying the burden of the world on your shoulders." She answered, "But I am. If I'm not home, everything goes wrong, and my sister has a fever, and I think it's because she knows she's not as gifted as I am...." She went on and on in that vein. It took awhile to prove to her that she was not responsible for her sister, that her parents were, and that adults would help her—myself, her teachers, and her parents.

I believe that gifted children need freedom to develop themselves, while they also need to feel protected by their parents. They need to be listened to, they need to be treated with a great deal of empathy and respect, and yet, at the same time, there needs to be no doubt about the fact that their parents are in charge and that they can rely on their parents to protect them, even though this may mean limiting them in many ways. Their unusual awareness exposes them soon enough to this confusing world; they must not be made to feel responsible for what goes on in their families.

While adults must be clear about maintaining their roles as parents or teachers, in a certain sense, they also become the peers of these children, because gifted children often cannot share their interests with other children. They speak a different language. They are interested in things that others of the same age are not interested in, such as a five-year-old who plays chess. One little boy I knew got very excited about the oil extracted from whales, and had some real basis for thinking that there was some unexplored medical uses for this oil. The other children were not interested in his speculations, and he needed to share his thoughts with an adult. So the adult needs to be the peer in many ways, but at the same time maintain the fact that he or she is an adult. Another little boy I worked with was absolutely outstanding in math. His father was a mathematician, and every day after school the two of them spent hours exploring mathematics together. It was a very happy kind of relationship between the two of them which did not in any way interfere with the fact that the father was the adult.

It is interesting that there is a tendency to feel that gifted children have more problems than others. It is my opinion that the environments of these children are more problematic than the children themselves. Their problems stem from the environment not understanding them, not giving them what they need, not fulfilling them. Actually, in many ways, gifted children are easier to handle than other children. They are very aware of the dangers in life, so they usually are more careful. It is not as likely that a gifted toddler will run into the street. It is not as likely that a gifted adolescent will experiment with drugs. These children are sometimes too afraid of kidnapping and illness and accidents, so they worry a great deal. However, they also have the ability to construct creative solutions to their problems. They have many inner resources and much information to rely on. If they are truly faced with a difficult situation, they probably would be more able to find a way out of it.

Most of all, gifted children are a delight. They are really very interesting people. They come up with so many unexpected ideas. In all these many years I have lived and worked with gifted children, my first reactions to them are feelings of delight, interest, and excitement. They are often basically well-adjusted children who are capable of concentrating for long periods, exploring and researching topics of interest to them.

How, then, can parents better understand and respond to the unique needs of their gifted children? It must be kept in mind that not only is every gifted child unique, but every parent-child relationship is also unique. Nevertheless, the following ten points elaborate things that all parents of gifted children should be aware of and do.

1. Accept your child's growth, which is a delight to watch, but remember that it is not a part of you. Your child's successes and failures belong to him or her alone. Your role is to help the child grow. This is more difficult than we think, because we have a tendency to identify with our children, to live through our children. This we do even more so with gifted children, who often feel that their gifts belong to their parents.

2. Do not compare your child with others or make other children's achievements milestones for him or her. This, too, is easier said than done, because we tend to accept and value normative behavior. If the neighbor's child is playing ball outside but your child is afraid to go out, or is more interested in playing the piano or doing whatever, then accept his or her wish to be different. If your child is not popular, or is not toilet-trained, resist the temptation to feel inferior and defensive about this or become angry at the child. Instead, allow

your child to develop at his or her own unique rate. Many differences in the gifted are quite positive, such as sensitivity, introversion, caution, avid reading, and intense interests. In order for your child to enjoy and be proud of his or her uniqueness, you need to support these differences.

3. Have empathy with your child's feelings of being different from other children. Gifted children often feel isolated. You can help them overcome this by finding other children who are like them and by being their friend. Adults often become the primary playmates of gifted children, and there is really nothing wrong with this. Most of all, gifted children need to feel that you understand them and will be the one to help them with those areas in which they are different from others.

4. Do not be in awe of your gifted child. Remain the person in charge, and allow your child to feel protected rather than giving the child the feeling that he or she is in charge. This happens more often than you might think. It seems like such a natural process, because gifted children often know more than we do, so slowly we turn decisions over to them. But to do so is not only unrealistic, it is also detrimental to the gifted child's growth.

5. Help your gifted child cope with perfectionism. At times, this means insisting that he or she try something new and risk failure. Certainly, it means teaching the child that every learning process includes failure. It also means supporting the child during periods of impatience and unhappiness that often precede important achievements.

6. Keep the channels of communication between you and your gifted child open. Always give your child the feeling that you are on his or her side, but do not intrude on the child's privacy. This also includes not overburdening gifted children with help doing things you know they are interested in. I have seen parents go out and buy lots of books on science and enroll their son in science courses once they found out that he was interested in science. This is fine, as long as the boy expresses a desire to have those books or enroll in those classes, but if the parents make those choices for him, he is likely to feel pressured into performing instead of encouraged to follow his own passions. As parents take over an activity or become active in it, their child may feel that something has been taken away from him or her. It is best to plan *with* children rather than for them.

7. Think about your philosophy of your role as parent. Gifted children have a global approach to things and need a large framework within which to effect their behaviors, decisions, actions, and plans. As the

person in charge, you need to be clear about your role in providing and managing this framework.

8. Become an advocate for your gifted child in the outside world. This is, I think, one of the most difficult tasks for parents of gifted children. Even though a great deal of progress has been made, the world does not readily accept the gifted. Teachers often feel threatened by them. Other people think they behave strangely. Gifted children feel like outsiders in such a world. Parents need to either find the appropriate learning environment for their gifted child or create one. Participate in parent support groups, try to change your child's school, and see to it that teachers are educated about all aspects of gifted children, even if they are not teaching a class for gifted children in particular. See to it that your child has a learning environment with the framework and freedom that he or she needs.

9. Build bridges to the outside world, thereby helping your child to learn skills that are needed to make that connection, but without hurting the development of his or her inner self. For instance, rather than saying, "You have to do this homework," even though you know that your child is not going to learn anything by doing it, you might say, "I know this homework is ridiculous, but I have no way of making it happen that you don't have to do it."

10. Realize that, in some ways, good education for gifted children is good education for *all* children. All children should have an individualized approach to education; all need to have their uniqueness understood and supported; all need support for the development of their emotions and inner selves. Most schools do not think of the development of the self. They do not even have a name for this. Schools usually have very narrowly defined goals and do not operate on the basis of a carefully thought-out philosophy. Meeting the needs of gifted children requires, above all, the right attitude toward the individual differences of the child. Does the school allow children to advance at their own rate, to pursue their own passions, and to interact with children with similar interests and abilities? If not, do everything you can to change this, to see to it that the needs of your gifted child are recognized and met.

I hope that my comments have helped to make parents more aware of the special challenges that gifted children pose, as well as the special sources of delight that they can be. It is also my hope that, in being more aware of these challenges and delights, they can become more supportive parents.

The Early Environment:
At Home and at School

A later version of this article appeared as a chapter titled "The Early Environment of the Child: Experience in a Continuing Search for Meaning" in *The Gifted Young in Science: Potential through Performance,* eds. Paul F. Brandwein and Harry A. Passau (Washington, D.C.: National Science Teachers' Association, 1988).

When a child is born, a learning, living environment creates itself; for it is from the child that all learning and growing originates. Not only are children their own original learning environments, but they also develop their own unique methods of learning.

What is the early environment at home and at school that encourages growth and learning in all young gifted children? It is the children themselves. When a child is born, a learning, living environment creates itself; for it is from the child that all learning and growing origi- nates. Not only are children their own original learning environments, but they also develop their own unique methods of learning. And as they do, they keep creating and adding to this environment that is uniquely their own and represents them. Thus, the learning environ- ment grows rapidly from tiny beginnings to a large space. This space is almost visible, especially in the case of gifted children. The impetus to learn, the process of it, and the sheer force of necessity behind it are awe-inspiring to watch. It is like an ever-increasing whirlpool of bub- bling water. Gifted children make their presence known.

In order to describe that environment, we must talk about the chil- dren themselves. Who are they? What are their characteristics? All human beings share many characteristics and needs, yet each is basi- cally different; and so gifted children experience the world in similar yet different ways. They are born with the same task: to master the world and make it their own. They are driven to learn physical and mental skills in order to build a foundation of trust in themselves and their environment. At no time in life is the motivation to learn and to understand as great as in early childhood. This learning is the study of science in the deepest sense, for what is science but the desire to create a structure from our experiences? This desire is as much of a basic need as food, love, and protection. In order to feel safe, children need to make sense of this strange chaos of sounds, sights, odors, touches, tastes, and all the other sensations and experiences around them.

From the beginning, the gifted show an even greater awareness of the complexities of the world, a greater desire to make sense of it all. They need to overcome the anxiety that results from this awareness by trying to bring order into the apparent chaos around them. They also have greater skills to deal with this task. In addition, they experience genuine pleasure and excitement from knowledge, information, and understanding. All this is part of the motivation for learning and the reason for the rapid growth that leads young children to acquire new skills daily. Their whole being concentrates on this intellectual, emotional, and physical task. Their intellectual ability helps them to explore and understand more sophisticated concepts, to increase their self-image, and allows them to cope with life in a variety of ways.

To live with young gifted children with well-developed selves is a pleasure and a challenge. Their minds work overtime. They soon exhaust their surroundings. They often master the necessary skills such as walking and talking more quickly. They often need little sleep and spend their waking hours learning or wanting to learn about life, death, the stars, and people. Even as young as age four, they worry about politics, the environment, justice, hunger in the world, fairness, animals, nature, the universe, baseball players, and many other things.

The tools for the acquisition of these facts and concepts are available to children from the beginning. How they are used differs with each child. One of the most important tools is play. Play has a structure and a purpose of its own. It contains risk-taking, repetition, change, touching, tasting, and many other things that help the child to discover. As time goes on, play grows in complexity, mastery, excitement, and fun, and children gain concepts and information through it. It is never just play, it is also growth. It is the way in which young children fulfill their passionate and absolute need for mastery.

Slowly, out of all this, certain experiences and concepts come into focus. At first children begin to have some kind of familiarity with daily rhythm and daily events. This may begin when they learn to know their mothers or their mothers' breasts. They may find that sucking sometimes stills hunger and sometimes doesn't. They start to realize that sucking the thumb satisfies but doesn't feed them. They may learn that when they cry, someone might come and pick them up. They soon learn that this happens when they hear footsteps, so they may stop crying when they hear them. After awhile, however, they may discover that some footsteps come to the crib but others pass it by. They begin to differentiate between a mother's footsteps and those of another person. They now stop crying only when their mothers enter and near their bed. Through this they have learned to understand that one certain event usually follows another, but only under certain circumstances. This is a sophisticated concept to learn. As they grow older, children learn that stairs are different from a flat area, that they can fall down them and get hurt. Thus they acquire their first lesson in science. Only a few years later, they will understand that they tumbled down the stairs because of the pull of gravity.

The children now grow by leaps and bounds in every way, each in his or her own manner. They exhibit physical mastery in activities such as walking, climbing, and all the types of movements, and intellectual mastery in talking, thinking, and other experiences. This includes learning elementary reading and science, which are usually considered academic work. They also begin to develop some ethical and social concepts, art ability, and physical ability. But most of all, as soon as they can talk, which is sometimes very early, they begin to ask many, many questions.

As they grow in understanding, mastery, and skills, they move through different developmental phases. Their world expands as more and more of the outside world becomes integrated as part of themselves, familiar and manageable. Every child does this in his or her own way. That is how we grow into different people with different characteristics. Being a young child means being, in the first place, a learner.

The amount of energy children expend on exploration and repetition has amazed generations of adults. To watch children encounter the world and their attempts to penetrate its structure and meaning is to watch good scientists at work. But they also sometimes lag behind because they soon see the complexities and the dangers surrounding them, and so they hold back. They may be the greatest explorers, but many of them also shrink from exploring the unknown.

Gifted children may learn skills differently from other children. They may be early readers yet late swimmers. Overall, their abilities help them to explore and understand more sophisticated concepts, increase or decrease their self-image, and cope with life in a variety of ways. They are likely to find more alternative solutions than others. They need to learn in order to understand so they can feel safe and can trust. According to Erik Erikson, learning to trust is the first great task of newborns. Understanding leads to trust, if they can find the world trustworthy. The task of adults is to make the world worthy of trust so that children, and therefore their learning environments, are safe.

All through this growth process, children are not alone. They are surrounded by family, teachers, society, fate, and many other factors. What are the ways in which we can support the natural growth and motivation of children? What can we do to work for their growth rather than against it? How do we maintain the freedom for children to grow from the inside out? They need to be understood. Children need to master the world as part of their self-growth, as part of developing their feelings of self and trust in themselves. But they can only trust themselves to reach out and grow if they feel loved, safe, and trusted by those around them. They can use their energy for exploration freely only if their surroundings allow them to. They will accept their own personalities only if they feel accepted by their surroundings. Just as they need to touch and play, they need to be touched, played with, and respected.

Parents of gifted children are more likely to see these children as extensions of themselves. Gifted children soon see this need in their parents and feel obligated to try to fulfill it. If children are seen as extensions of the parents' selves, if they have to fulfill needs of their parents that have so far gone unfulfilled, they do not feel safe and cannot fulfill their own needs. If, for instance, parents want their four-year-old daughter to show everyone who enters the house how well she can read, her reading ability becomes the parents' success and fulfills their need to be outstanding, not hers. On the other hand, if the child does not do well, or is not interested in reading, this becomes her failure. Soon the child starts to feel that her parents will love her only if she can be a success for them. The parents need the child to make up for their own lack of success, and the child becomes the "I love you only if you fulfill my needs" child. As she disappoints them, she will disappoint herself.

In this type of situation, even very young children will not have their energies free for exploration of their world. The young girl of our example feels hindered by anger, anxiety, and inner restrictions. Failure becomes dangerous in terms of losing her parents' love. She will begin to look outside of herself to figure out how she should behave in order to please her parents and fulfill their expectations.

Therefore, the first condition for creating an appropriate environment for learning is that parents must see their children as separate persons who own themselves, their own growth, their own successes, and their own failures. They need love, protection, and guidance until they can protect and guide themselves and incorporate the love of their parents. These things can happen only when parents allow their children to grow. If we praise them and give them recognition for success and growth in their own terms, they will feel accepted and understood.

They will feel like insiders in this world. Many, many children, but especially the gifted, suffer from a feeling of being outsiders, of not being understood, not being able to communicate their real selves and needs.

Parents who are free from their own needs have the empathy to sense what children require at a particular moment. This is one of adults' most difficult tasks. Children may require more freedom to explore in one instance, and need more guidance and protection in another. It is important that there be a clear-cut difference between allowing children to grow and treating them as though they were already grown up. They cannot yet take responsibility for their lives. Their freedom can only exist within the security of adult leadership. Children need the protection of knowing that parents are in charge, that there are clear-cut rules and regulations, and that adults make decisions in terms of their children and for their sake, but that children do not necessarily make decisions. One of the difficulties of raising gifted children is for parents to sense when they need to withdraw and turn the power to make decisions over to their children. Parents of the gifted often stand in awe of their children and find it hard to remain adults in that situation. At times, the family revolves around these children and their interests and concerns, and the children develop an unrealistic view of their role in the family. They see themselves as different from others, not governed by the same rules that govern others. They consider themselves adults and feel that they have adult rights and responsibilities. In fact, this makes them anxious and insecure. Such children maintain a position that they know to be untenable and is therefore frightening, rather than using their energy for growing and learning.

Children are surrounded not only by their families but also by society as a whole, and are exposed to society's expectations and traditions. Expectations and desires flow from children to the outside world, but they also flow in the other direction. The world expects something from them, just as they expect something from the world. To others, they are part of the outside world, just as others are part of the outside world to them. The flow towards them influences and changes the direction of their growth. This can be either supportive and continue growth in the same direction to create a river of learning and growing, or it can move in the other direction to divert and at times to slow the river down to a trickle or dry it up altogether.

Society's expectations come from the outside in. We have developed certain goals and expectations and certain methods of achieving them. We expect children to adapt to these. We measure their responses in terms of them. Children reach their goals of mastery through many, many different avenues. Society only allows a few. We have established definite sequences. We have decided what, how, and when they will learn. We have decided what constitutes success. We think in terms of outer success. But children think and feel in terms of mastery, which means inner success. Children become acceptable to society only if the world sees them succeed on its own terms.

Society has also decided on the method through which children are to learn—they are to be taught, and they are to passively receive this teaching—when in fact children learn actively by participating, by experiencing with their whole body, their whole being. Children do not all learn in the same way, at the same time, or at the same age. More often than not, we interfere with their basic motivation for learning and their basic goal for learning by destroying their budding creativity and crippling the natural flow and development of their growth. We need to recognize and respect the basic learning environment that already exists, namely, the children themselves. We need to recognize that there is a legitimate reason for children's unique interests and ways of learning. We need to find ways to expand the original learning environment to create a climate of trust and support, and provide opportunities for growth.

In what climate does the needed trust grow best? Children who are allowed to grow freely develop some very specific, unusual interests and knowledge. They may acquire information and knowledge for which they need recognition and praise, but in reality they more often receive a smile of disbelief. This is particularly true for the unique interests of the young gifted. For example, I have met some three- to five-year-olds who want to know exactly how toilets work or the sewer system functions. Some collect roots or food stamps. One child wants to know how door knobs function. Some children love to take machines and radios apart and put them back together again. There are probably millions of interests and activities that little children have which, as a rule, are not allowed to develop and express themselves. The little rocks on the way to the museum may be more exciting to a child than the beautiful displays in the museum itself. The rocks were his discovery. Some of these interests may be strange, but they are all stepping-stones toward mastery and growth and should be allowed to blossom.

These interests and fascinations usually correspond to children's developmental phases. The three-year-old who has just been toilet-trained is reluctant to give up his bowel movement and the flushing disappearance of it frightens him. To understand how the toilet functions and where its contents go means acquiring familiarity and intellectual mastery, which leads to acceptance and emotional mastery. Finding out means taking in, incorporating. Knowing how doors open relieves anxiety about being separated, about people leaving, about feeling shut into a room. It grows out of a need to learn how to cope emotionally with an anxiety-producing situation, but it takes the form of intellectual understanding of the situation. Knowing how doors open and close, how they look, how the hinges work, what different types of doors there are, and what the purpose of doors is leads to a familiarity that helps to integrate the situation.

An interest in dinosaurs or roots expresses children's need to understand where they came from, to understand the past and the future. Children want to know about origins. They want to know about where they themselves come from, how babies are made and born, why boys and girls are different. They want to know why adults usually change the subject and seem to close their ears when questions about sex are asked. This is one area where adults, for their own reasons, want to stop the flow of inquiry on the part of children. As a rule, we applaud children when they show interest and want to know about things, but when it comes to sex, the message children get says, "No trespassing." This reaction in itself often becomes a hindrance to the natural curiosity of young children. They sense that some areas are forbidden territory and that certain questions must not be asked. They begin to feel that some doors are not open to them. For children, interest in sex is part of their desire to understand the world. In fact, it is a very important part of that desire. I believe that we should give children information about sex as soon as they show signs of interest in it, which may not necessarily take the form of direct questions, for they sense the parents' reluctance even without asking.

Many young children are preoccupied with death. Here again, they try to solve this emotional need to feel safe through the intellect. What is death like? What happens to our feelings when we die? One gifted four-year-old girl attempted not to move at all for a whole day in an attempt to understand what death feels like. In many cases, such concerns and questions are the starting point for ever-widening interests in many directions. For instance, wanting to know about death grows into an interest about nature, living beings, or the environment. I know gifted children, four years old and older, who can name every part of the body and its function and who have a passionate interest in it. This overwhelming interest originated with questions about the differences between life and death and what inanimate objects are. Out of this grew a preoccupation with all living things and their different physical characteristics. This, then, developed into very accurate knowledge of the human body. Other young children may move into a different direction such as religion and ask questions about the nature of God, whether Santa Claus is real, whether there is life after death, and so on.

Part of the desire for mastery and protection develops into a need to understand the ethical framework of the interactions between people. Children want to understand the reasons for the rules and regulations that govern our lives. Many gifted children have a deep sense of justice. They want to know what is right and wrong and why. Unfairness makes them feel unsafe, because that makes the basic rules unrecognizable. Just as they need a structure of the world in general, they need a structure of the basic concepts of ethics. Every subject matter should include the opportunity to ask ethical questions concerning its content. Children are concerned with the moral questions that arise out of global interdependence, technological growth, and everyday human relations. But ethical questions are often avoided in the regular classroom for fear of entering politics or becoming controversial.

One specific characteristic of gifted children is their perfectionism. This sometimes interferes with their motivation for learning and exploration, and requires special consideration in our approach to helping them learn. They become most impatient if they do not succeed in a self-imposed task, such as drawing a horse the way they see it. It is difficult for them to accept that their fine motor control does not keep up with their sophisticated ideas. This desire to be perfect often has the effect of keeping gifted children from exposing themselves to failure. Helping them to understand that failure is part of growth, that possibly their expectations of themselves are unrealistic, and assisting them in reaching their goals are some of the ways in which adults can help children to cope with this particular difficulty. Perfectionism brings with it a fear of risk-taking and this, again, stands in the way of gifted children exposing themselves to new growth. They need encouragement and a background of support in order to have the courage to try something new, even though they are not sure that they can really achieve it.

Many gifted children do not care about grades, honors, or awards, although parents' or teachers' expectations may lead them in that direction against their real inner needs. They may be faced with a dichotomy between their real interests and outside pressures that create internal conflicts. Although the gifted enjoy competition in specific areas, they are, in general, not interested in competition and feel more free to grow without a competitive approach. Freedom from competition allows them to pursue their own very original interests, which may not be shared by anybody else and therefore are not subject to competition. Many gifted children truly want to climb the mountain because it is there, not because it means they will have achieved success.

With gifted children, even more than with others, the emphasis must be on learning, what they take in, how they digest it, and how they use it rather than on teaching. They want to do their own learning just as scientists want to do their own research.

What is the best school environment for gifted children? Their eagerness to make the world their own soon grows beyond the confines of the home. They need to venture out and relate to adults other than their parents and expand their opportunities to grow. Some children are ready for a small group experience at age one-and-a-half. But the gifted may have a harder time separating from home because of the greater awareness of the big step they are taking. This transition requires great support and empathy from parents. The children need to be given time to learn to feel safe in their new environment. They need a familiar person around while they begin to relate to others. They need to know that the mother trusts the new adult so that they can transfer some of their feelings of safety to an environment away from home. If this move creates a loss of security, impairment of the self follows and withdrawal of energy from learning and growing takes place because these resources must now be used for self-protection.

We must remember that children in this new situation remain the same people with the same characteristics and needs as the people they are at home. They need to be protected, loved, and respected. A personal relationship to the teacher is necessary before they can become a partic-ipating and secure member of a group. One essential factor in this personal relationship is the teacher's recognition of and respect for their individual methods of learning, interests, and goals. Play and explo-ration remain the best learning tools for young children. They develop a sense of inner freedom and permission to reach out if their goals and methods are supported and cherished by the adults of the school. This requires a flexible atmosphere peopled by stimulating, enthusiastic adults who are themselves learners, and much opportunity for discov-ery, individualized and group learning, and play.

Gifted children need adults who will open doors for them with their own knowledge, resources, and desires to learn, but who will not try to push them through those doors. These adults constitute the first trusting relationship as parent substitutes outside the home. As children grow through developmental phases, they often develop similar interests which, once discovered by a teacher, can be used as a basis for common learning experiences. For example, they may be interested in learning about dinosaurs or about how things work. They might like to know what being alive means, or to learn what is real and what is pretend, or grasp the difference between animate and inanimate objects. These things are basic to the developing structure of children's worlds. To understand the difference between reality and fantasy allows them to cope better with each. This knowledge creates the opportunity for safe expression of normal hostility in fantasy without having to fear any real-istic consequences. Learning about the laws of the physical world around them serves as a basis from which they will develop further understandings. Therefore, children often exhibit great enthusiasm toward learning about physical or natural sciences in an atmosphere of discovery.

Nursery schools more often than grade schools offer this type of atmosphere. Traditionally, they have been more attuned to the developmental phases and the needs of individual children or groups of children, and provide appropriate experiences in cognitive learning as well as opportunities for social learning and interaction and creative expression within a flexible, open environment. Children in such groups maintain their passion for learning. In this approach, the teacher becomes the facilitator. The emphasis is on learning, not teaching. In such an environment there is a clear-cut, well thought out philosophy of helping children move toward self-actualization. Children are encouraged to use their real potential to develop an approach to life rather than pursue the narrow goals of acquiring traditional skills and going to college. Skills are necessary as tools, but not as an end in themselves, and an education that supports inner motivation and fosters the potential for learning is based on goals and methods that are fundamentally different from traditional ones.

Child-Centered Educational Approach	Traditional Educational Approach
Education for life, self-actualization	Education for college, financial gains, or success
Emphasis on the whole child	Emphasis on academics and sports only
Learning	Teaching
Discovery, inquiry method, active learning	Facts, passive intake
Learning to make choices	Rigid curriculum
Freedom within a framework	Traditional learning goals and methods taken for granted, pressure
Concern with developmental phases	Skill development based on age and grade level
Complex conceptualization based on many causes, many effects	Linear curriculum
Children define themselves	Society defines the children

Gifted children are global thinkers. They want to understand the whole before learning about details. They need to understand the overall concept before they learn detailed facts. For example, I once observed children being taught the names of different types of dogs. They learned them mechanically because they did not understand what dogs are really like. The gifted need to begin with an overall concept of dogs as mammals and animals and *then* learn about the differences among them within this framework.

As children grow older, the amount of possible information and learning opportunities becomes overwhelming for them. What is the task of the teacher in that case? In addition to what I have described earlier, the teacher must make opportunities for learning available to children and build bridges to society's expectations without interfering with their self-directedness. The unit approach can provide a structure that makes information manageable without limiting the potential for discovery. In the child-centered approach, such a unit often grows out of discussions between children and teachers, and therefore represents the children's real interests. A unit that develops out of the questions asked by children and that includes their approach to finding the answers allows individuals or groups of children to continue to create their own environment. This approach illustrates the contrast between the child-centered and the traditional approaches to education, for the curriculum of the traditional elementary school is usually rigidly predetermined rather than developed through cooperation between the general goals of the teacher and children's individual ones.

In the traditional approach, textbooks are the basis of teaching, while in the child-centered approach textbooks provide useful resources or a usable background. The curriculum of the elementary school is usually based on skill learning. But the gifted are concept learners, often with specific interests in science or social studies, and their approach to learning is the inquiry method. Neither these areas of study nor this approach are central in elementary education. Very little science is taught in elementary school. Often it is restricted to handouts, workbooks, and the occasional cooking experiences. The curriculum for gifted children—indeed for all children—should be based primarily on concept learning, with skills seen as tools necessary to achieve these goals. If concept learning through social studies or science were the center of elementary education, many gifted children would be able to share their amazing fund of knowledge with others and feel an accepted part of the community. However, this opportunity usually does not exist. This is a loss to them and to the other children.

Gifted children are often daydreamers. Many ideas and much inspiration come to them while they are lost in thought. This is not understood and is frowned upon by the adults around them. It is considered a problem. Gifted children make friends with the opposite sex or with those who act a little different from others and who are also gifted. They may share specific or varied interests. Often, such friendships are laughed at, and further collaboration and common discoveries are made impossible. For the gifted, the world is not divided into small subjects. They learn concepts that apply to many subjects at the same time. A co-curricular approach and flexible grouping with a flexible classroom is appropriate for them. Gifted children need opportunities to make choices, to work with a variety of adults who may be experts in specific fields, and to complete tasks to which they are passionately committed rather than being disrupted to concentrate on something else. As they grow older, they live with the increasing pressure of their multiple talents and interests. They need opportunities for the creative expression of their ideas through communication and discussion as well as more traditional avenues of creative expression. Few such opportunities exist. If art, music, drama, dance, and other artistic expressions are considered frills in the school environment, if they have low priority and are eliminated as soon as money is tight, the gifted will not only lack the opportunity to grow and fulfill their potential but will also be hurt emotionally.

Why do children in general seem to lose their motivation to learn by the time they are about eight years old? What happens between the time when the child was driven to learn and this age? What experiences create this change? Could it be caused by the goals and methods of the child being at cross-purposes with the goals and methods of traditional education? Instead of investigating this phenomenon, education seems to accept it as a natural fact and replaces natural motivation with artificial ones such as grades, rewards, punishment, disappointment, and competition. Gifted children suffer even more from the discrepancy between their own expectations and those of society. They feel misunderstood, deprived of opportunities for growth, stifled. They react to this situation with depression, aggression, and misbehavior. Conversely, in programs where approaches that support their needs and methods are used, where scientific concepts and the study of the world are at the center of the curriculum rather than on the periphery or are altogether avoided, children are highly motivated, knowledgeable, and happy. Many children have been brought to me because their schools have considered them problems. In my opinion, most of these children are not problem children. It is their environment that has created a problem for them.

Children are their own learning environments, and growth takes place if we take this as the basis for our approach to education.

Issues in Gifted Child Education

Published under the title "The Role and Responsibility of Organizations in Gifted Child Education" in the journal of the Michigan Academy for Gifted (August, 1986), an organization founded by Roeper Schools, Oakland Public Schools, and Oakland University in Michigan.

My personal opinion is that we need to emphasize much more the global aspects of education, the skills of cooperation, peaceful conflict resolution, and practical ways in which our gifted children can grow up to make an impact on the world.

The interest of the educational community in gifted education has gone through several phases. It was awakened by Lewis Terman's long-term study of the gifted, which was the first to focus attention on the characteristics and needs of the gifted. After that, interest waned somewhat until the event of *Sputnik* and the belief that the gifted would enable us to compete with Russia. From that time on, there have continued to be some swings of the pendulum in terms of awareness of the needs of the gifted. The movement has never completely disappeared, however. It changed in emphasis from the idea that the gifted are the nation's best resources to the belief that the gifted have the civil right to have their specific needs recognized, understood, and fulfilled.

The impetus for this came from the interaction of a variety of factors and groups. Universities began to become more aware of the gifted. Individuals became interested in doing research on the gifted. Teachers started to understand some of the phenomena they experienced in the classroom with these children. Parents began to see that their children's characteristics had to be interpreted within a different framework than that of the established norm, namely, within the framework of gifted children themselves.

Out of this awareness grew a network of professional and parent organizations. Research was carried out, published, and disseminated in the form of books, journals, and articles. Organizations grew locally, then nationally, and finally internationally. Schools and programs developed. In turn, these organizations and programs had an impact on their environment in terms of public acceptance and understanding of the needs of the gifted. I believe that the most important role of organizations has been to legitimize gifted education.

There has always been the same difficulty to be overcome, namely, the public resistance to the whole concept of gifted child education. This originated from a generally misunderstood concept of democracy and a fear of elitism. Out of this grew many other related concerns. People felt that the parents of gifted children were only living out their own ambitions. They felt that money needed for other children would be siphoned off for the exclusive benefit of the gifted. There was fear that those who were already endowed with more financial resources than others would be given even more support. Added to this was the apprehension and even the fear of the powers and abilities of gifted children. Organizations for the gifted offered a forum in which to debate all of these questions and helped people become knowledgeable on the topic of the gifted. This has brought with it a much greater acceptance of gifted child education. It has clarified many questions and cleared away many of the myths.

I have been able to follow the development of the understanding of gifted child education most closely in Michigan, particularly in the Detroit area. I have also become familiar with the approach to the gifted in other states and countries. From this I have learned that debates about the gifted usually begin with concern about elitism and go on from there to a variety of subjects. Once it is understood that the concept of democracy and universal education means serving the needs of each and all, many people learn to see the gifted as one of the groups to be served rather than the elite. The next step is usually an interest in identifying and naming the characteristics of the gifted. This is followed by a desire to discuss parental roles, learning environments, peer relationships, and methods of evaluation, and continues with the expansion of the concept of giftedness to include the creatively gifted, the learning disabled gifted, and the emotional development of the gifted. The more knowledgeable people allow themselves to become on the subject, the more acceptable it becomes to them and to the community. After awhile, this information becomes eagerly sought.

It became apparent to me that, after the gifted child movement had been alive in Michigan for a number of years, groups who asked me to speak to them had become much more sophisticated and were looking for information beyond how to identify and characterize the gifted. It was particularly encouraging when the subject of emotional development became of interest to my Michigan and national audiences. Up until that point, I felt that this important area had not reached the consciousness of people working with gifted children. When I spoke in other places, I often felt that the background that I could assume in Michigan was not yet present in other areas.

A combination of factors have made Michigan a forerunner in gifted child education. This includes the development of the Academy for Gifted, with its unique basis of public, private, and university connections, and the fact that the Roeper City and Country School became a school for the gifted as early as 1956. Through the possibility of observing gifted child education at the Roeper School, people became aware that giftedness is not dangerous and that the gifted are human beings like everybody else, but that they also have specific needs. Since then, two other private schools for the gifted—the Gibson School and Emerson School—have opened in the Detroit area, and many other programs for the gifted have been started in the public schools. The programs for gifted children in the Detroit public school system make it unique among the nation's school systems.

The concept was spread further as more and more colleges in Michigan began to teach gifted child education in many different ways. Consequently, planning for the gifted has become more and more integrated into educational planning all throughout the nation. This means that more and more people look to professional organizations to educate them about the needs of the gifted, which places an enormous responsibility on leaders in the field. As the public becomes more sophisticated and learns more about gifted child education, they expect more innovative answers and ideas.

Education, with some exceptions, has kept itself in splendid isolation from the social and political events of the moment. I feel that the time has come to reevaluate this position in light of the danger of complete destruction of our planet. For educators of the gifted, however, this has become an even more immediate question. We have made gifted child education visible to the world. Now different sectors are taking notice and are beginning to realize the great resource that they have in the gifted. Businesses, scientific fields, the military, and NASA are all vying for the gifted. NASA now offers scholarships in curricula to the gifted child movement. The peace movement offers peace curricula to all educational institutions. And the establishment of a Peace Academy is being planned in the United States Congress.

The gifted child movement is surrounded by all these activities. Can the movement really isolate itself from these concerns? Is neutrality in these matters a responsible stand to take? Do we not unwittingly become involved by responding to pressures from outside? Do we want to be known, for instance, as supporters of the Strategic Defense Initiative (SDI) or of the peace movement? Debate on these questions is urgently needed. We must look at the issues openly and decide where our responsibilities lie.

My personal opinion is that we need to emphasize much more the global aspects of education, the skills of cooperation, peaceful conflict resolution, and practical ways in which our gifted children can grow up to make an impact on the world.

At the moment, however, I feel that the answer to the question of where we will put our support must be superseded by the question of our moral responsibility to take a stand as educators of the gifted. The Academy for the Gifted has been a leader in the past. Can it also become a leader in opening this debate?

Should Educators of the Gifted and Talented Be More Concerned With World Issues?

Presented at the Eighth World Conference of the World Council for Gifted and Talented Children, Salt Lake City, Utah (August, 1987).

Education does not exist in isolation. We are part of an overall network of relationships and interdependence.

Gifted education has come of age. It has become legitimate and it is here to stay. This conference, the Eighth World Conference for Gifted and Talented, bears witness to this. I have been able to follow the movement since its infancy. It can be proud of itself. It was difficult for the educational community and the general public to accept the fact that the gifted have special needs. Retarded and handicapped children obviously need help, but in the past the general opinion was that the gifted are overprivileged by nature. It took great dedication by many people to make the needs of the gifted visible. So many obstacles had to be overcome: How do we identify the gifted? Who are they? What are their educational needs? How do they differ? How can one provide for them? The next issue was how to accommodate the creative child within the concept of the gifted. We also grappled with the question of how the gifted are emotionally different from others. At a certain point, psychologists, counselors, and psychiatrists began to become knowledgeable about the gifted. The needs of the gifted in different socioeconomic groups, ethnic groups, and countries became evident.

Through the efforts of this organization, the needs of the gifted all over the world became visible and recognizable. From the general public came the concern with elitism, the concern that helping the gifted was undemocratic. For a while, the driving force behind gifted education was the notion that the gifted are the greatest resource of a country. This was followed by the recognition that it is the civil right of gifted children, as

168

it is the civil right of all children, to have their educational needs fulfilled. I believe that even though there is still much left to be done, gifted child education is now recognized as a legitimate part of the educational scene. To reach this point required looking inside ourselves and concentrating on achieving these different goals. They were achieved through lively debate and research.

Now the time has come to open a new area of debate, to begin research in a different direction, and to emphasize a different area in our conferences, meetings, and publications. This area may possibly be the most difficult of all.

One of the well-known characteristics of the gifted is their enormous sense of justice. Gifted children are questioners, keen observers, logical thinkers. They notice inequities, unfairness, and double standards and question them with passion. Often they feel helpless and powerless to make an impact, and they suffer deeply from this fact. They notice these kinds of problems in the family, the community, and the world. They worry about peace, about the bomb, about their futures, about the environment, about all the problems that they encounter. But as a rule we do not help or support them in their questioning or help them to cope with this. Debate on ethical questions is actually taboo in many parts of the educational community, or if it is not taboo, it is avoided. The educational community keeps itself in splendid isolation. It is afraid of being criticized if it ventures into these areas. It is afraid of being accused of having entered the political realm. So children are left alone in their struggle with these concerns.

In an atmosphere in which the environment is open to small and large questions of justice in the world, it is amazing how these questions are forthcoming from children at every opportunity. In open discussion groups at the Roeper City and Country School in Michigan, the first thing that children would talk about was their concern for safety in the world, or, for example, their concern for parents who could not give up smoking. In most institutions, however, the atmosphere creates a different type of emphasis. The person who unquestioningly accepts the status quo, who sticks to the rules no matter whether they are fair or not, is viewed as acceptable. Children learn that they are expected not to rock the boat or question existing hierarchies. They are to be obedient either because that is deemed "good behavior" or because adults view it as impossible to change.

In such cases a subculture often develops, especially among the gifted. They learn how to beat the system, how to get around the rules. They learn how to impress adults in the way they know adults want to be impressed. Ethical considerations are not emphasized, so they do these things for personal gain. They learn that might makes right, that to think in any other way is to be an idealist whose head is in the clouds, who is not "down to earth." I must make it clear that I am not speaking of everyone at every school. But I am speaking of the majority. I am speaking of what I have observed, seen, read, and heard from children.

As a rule, there is little or no debate on such questions as:

- Should decisions be made on the basis of personal goals?
- When does obedience stop being ethical?
- Is the majority always ethically right?
- Is team spirit always the final deciding factor?
- What is loyalty? Is it always ethically right?
- Does the end justify the means?
- On what principles do we base our decisions?
- How do we make our decisions?
- Do we look at problems from all sides?

Here I would like to stress that I am not saying that we provide children with answers to these questions to impress upon them our own convictions and dogmatic answers. Rather, these areas should be open to debate and question. There should be a forum in which the emphasis on and importance of curriculum, classes, and opportunities as part of their education can be discussed. We need to give children the opportunity to think about what their role in the world should be, what impact they can make and want to make, and what impact the world has on their lives. They need the tools to make an impact on their own destinies and the ever-expanding interrelatedness of the destinies of others on the planet.

Why is this so important? First, because we are neglecting an important need within our gifted children and all children; and second, because the individual does not grow up in isolation. Education does not exist in isolation. We are part of an overall network of relationships and interdependence. Because of their own needs and what they as gifted individuals have to offer, children need to understand this fact and learn how to live with it. They are growing up in a world beset with problems created by technical advances, both constructive and destructive. They will be called upon to make ethical decisions in whatever careers they choose to pursue. They will have to make decisions about mercy killing, when a person is considered legally dead, abortion, world hunger, world peace, and environmental problems. These considerations are important for education everywhere in the world and for all children, because all are touched by them in different ways. But the gifted, in particular, are affected by them. I believe that there is a basic set of world issues and problems that influences each country and each person in a different way. In all countries, it will be the gifted who will make an impact and may be able to bring about change. And it may be the gifted young people who can learn about each other and be of help to one other.

But in order for this to happen, we must admit to ourselves that merely recognizing and supporting giftedness is in itself not enough. We must admit to ourselves that giftedness is neither a virtue nor a vice, but that the gifted have the enormous potential to become more virtuous or more vicious than the average person. They may be the ones who will save this world, but they also have the capacity to destroy it. We hear about both valiant and destructive human efforts every day in the media. When we look at the people involved in destructive events, we find that those who are the most destructive are the intellectual giants and the ethical morons. They have been given educational opportunities to learn, but not the same opportunities for moral and ethical growth. In this sense, we educators of the gifted bear a great worldwide responsibility. We can participate in educating people who have the intellectual and ethical capacity to understand and unravel the problems of the world. We can also participate in educating people who have the capacity to destroy it because their intellectual capacity is not supported by ethical capacity. I believe that we have an enormous responsibility and that we need to recognize this fact and focus on it, even though it may bring us into certain conflicts and demand courageous action from us.

It seems to me that before we can try to work with our gifted children in this respect, each and every individual educator must make a decision in terms of his or her own ethical obligations toward the world. One of the reasons ethical education does not play a role in the daily program of schools is because it does not play a significant role in the daily lives of the adults. We are so concerned with living that we often do not think about *how* to live. It is for these reasons that I hope we can find ways to focus on these issues and give them much consideration in future meetings, in research and debate, in the classroom, and in our own lives.

Empathy, Ethics, and Global Education

Published in *Understanding Our Gifted,* vol. 1, no. 6 (July, 1989), pp. 1, 7–10.

We are at a point in the history of our planet where it has become a necessity to become globally aware. We need to understand our interconnectedness in every facet of living— our private lives, politics, education, economics, law, medicine, and everything else. This knowledge alters our way of life and our way of educating children.

Global education means understanding the totality of interdependence. Interdependence is an unalterable fact of life for everything on this earth as well as in the whole universe. The calcium that is now in our bodies was created billions of years ago by some turbulent events in the universe. A book written in England leads to a death threat in Iran that resounds all around the world. We are deeply immersed in an interdependent network. Our well-being, our very existence, depends on the microcosm of our bodies, including their cells and bacteria, and the macrocosm of the rays of the sun and the universe beyond. For this reason, all of our actions affect others who affect others and, in the end, affect us again. Ecology of behavior is a reality that seems self-evident but about which we may not yet be aware. It has not been incorporated in our emotions, thoughts, activities, and way of life. We have not really incorporated the concept that the world and everything in it, animate and inanimate, are completely dependent upon one another. Nothing happens or exists that does not have an impact on something else. It is thus a matter of survival to think in terms of global responsibility.

Empathy

We are at a point in the history of our planet where it has become a necessity to become globally aware. We need to understand our interconnectedness in every facet of living—our private lives, politics, education, economics, law, medicine, and everything else. This knowledge alters our way of life and our way of educating children. To incorporate this reality, we need not only to know it, but also to feel it. We need to feel our connection with others and view others as a part of ourselves. We need to develop global empathy. Only then can we begin to act on this knowledge and teach it to our children. We need to try to feel the world—its beauty, its sorrow, its suffering, its conflicts. This means the planet and everything on it—the plants, the animals, the environment, and the people.

We know about different cultures, but do we know how it *feels* to grow up in a different culture? How does it feel to grow up in South Africa, in Russia, in South America, in different parts of our own country, during a war, with a different religious background, or with different economic circumstances? How does it feel to be homeless? Today we know more about different countries, different people and their experiences, and global events. Television has opened the world to us to a much larger extent. We watched the massacre at Beijing on the news. We know about it, but do we feel it? Or are we overwhelmed with so much suffering and turmoil that we have lost the ability to empathize by the time we become adults?

Do children have empathy? Yes, they do. Children are new to this world. Each experience is fresh and three-dimensional—lived through with soul, mind, and body. It becomes part of them and they feel it deeply. Gifted children show great empathy for others in many different ways. They cry at sad stories or movies. They become very emotionally involved and feel strongly for themselves and others. Even though they may be jealous of a sibling, they cannot stand it when they see their brother or sister punished at home, or when they see similar things done to others at school. I have witnessed gifted children refuse to tease other children or do anything that is hurtful to other children or animals. This does not mean, of course, that they never have hostile feelings or express them in aggressive behavior. But they are often the ones who will, for example, befriend the child who is strange.

Helena Deutsch, a psychoanalyst who wrote a great deal about gifted people, once said, "The gifted have a love affair with the world." It was her theory that the gifted extend feelings of love and empathy beyond the personal environment, that they have the ability to truly experience the world. In other words, the gifted have a greater capacity for empathy and can empathize with a greater number of people.

It is my belief that what begins as empathy in children develops into a value system in adults. It is the task of the modern educator to keep alive this global empathy and help develop the value systems of our gifted children and all children. This requires that we, as adults, enhance our own global awareness; only then we can help children develop their ethical values and value systems. The concept of global empathy represents a new point of view for us. Humankind's problem has been that it has been separated from this awareness in the past and, therefore, has developed along a path that is contrary to reality. Our feeling, and therefore, our thinking, is directed toward our own limited goals rather than an understanding of our interconnectedness. This leads us to act against the laws of interdependence.

Interdependence

An interdependent model of thinking requires a completely different focus—a different way of living, feeling, thinking, learning, teaching, and conceptualizing. For example, for centuries we have deforested our landscape and interrupted the ecosystem with disastrous results. Now we are about to destroy the ecology by deforestation of the rain forests. Events such as these are not single events, but are consequences of our noninterdependent attitudes and ways of thinking. Ecologists and environmentalists have attempted to increase our awareness; however, we are still functioning in our old modes of thinking and feeling.

The lack of interdependent thinking skills leads to many of the great problems and tragedies in the world. Interdependent thought looks at cause and effect as if they were many pebbles thrown into a pond. Each creates an ever-widening circle; the circles criss-cross one another but follow a logical pattern and structure. Natural laws of interdependence are being discovered in ecology, heredity, and many other fields. These laws can also be found in the structure of human relations, communities, and trade. Laws of interdependence exist in all areas, but some have not yet been discovered. The task of the present is to learn about the interdependence of human relations.

Interdependent thought changes many concepts which have been taken for granted. Let us examine the concept of personal success, for example. The traditional concept of personal success grows from the concept of competition, for personal success means being better than others. Success within the framework of interdependence would be defined as responsible participation in society, not as popularity, power, or financial earnings. Success in this context is *shared* success. The concept of competition, although not excluded, would be replaced by the concept of cooperation as the moving force of our thought and behavior.

Survival of the fittest would be replaced by survival of the planet, for the fittest is interdependently involved and could not survive without the planet. Nationalism would be redefined as helping and cooperating rather than competing, as pride in the compassion of one's country rather than in its comparative strength. The arms race is a typical example of lack of interdependent thought and planning, for the more weapons one country produces, the more others try to acquire them, too. Therefore, with each additional weapon we increase our national insecurity. Our politics and priorities would be fundamentally different if we thought interdependently. In the context of schools, interdependence means redefining our conceptions of learning and motivation. We must realize that everything has multiple causes and effects. Most of our lives are dominated by linear thinking: we think and act as if there were a single cause and a single effect.

Human beings need a community to which they belong in order to feel safe and comfortable. The traditional structure of a community—including the school community—is based on a hierarchy. An interdependent community is based on a cooperative, participatory democracy rather than a hierarchy. A hierarchy assumes a top and a bottom, a loser and a winner. Yet we all know the top depends on the bottom and vice versa. We need to understand that we are part of large entities. We live in a community which is part of the state, part of the country, part of the continent, and part of the world. Communities and nations, as well as people, are interdependent and can only coexist satisfactorily if they learn to cooperate with one another.

Ethics

Ethical behavior must also be reevaluated within the concept of interdependence. The ethics of interdependence differs basically from the ethics of obedience. The ethics of obedience grow out of hierarchical thinking; they say, in effect, that it is ethical to do as you are told by those in power. Schools expect this type of obedience. Children are called "responsible" if they obey the rules and the authorities. But obedience does not in actuality teach responsibility; it relieves individuals of the burden of responsibility since they do not have to think for themselves. There are, of course, other reasons why we often choose to do what others tell us to. We do so, for instance, when we trust their expertise and believe that they will act on our behalf. This is not the same thing as blind obedience, however, because we use our own judgment to decide whom to trust.

Ethics, in terms of interdependence, are universal and make an impact on others. Universal ethics are based on equal human rights and equal human responsibility. Out of this framework grows all ethical behavior. Because we depend on each other, we have to learn to trust and to be trustworthy. This means that we may not use each other for our own purposes. Abuse of this principle is one of the basic causes of distrust and hostility.

Children suffer from the abuse of trust. If, for instance, the demand for a popular teacher is so great that not all children can be accommodated in her room, it is most likely that the child who is excluded will not be the child of the board member. The reality may be that another child is much more in need of this particular teacher than the daughter of the board member. This, then, is an example of decisions being made on some basis other than need. Out of such actions grow resentment and alienation.

Self-Actualization

To live in an interdependent society means developing self-actualizing individuals at home and at school. A newborn child is dependent and develops self-esteem based on the love of his or her parents. As the child grows older, the traditional model supports this feeling of dependency. You are regarded as a worthwhile person if you win, if you are popular, if you receive good grades, or if you behave well. These are the messages that our children receive from those in charge of their lives. From an interdependent perspective, however, we recognize each child's inherent value. Each one of us brings something to this world from the moment we are born. We bring something unique that needs recognition to blossom and to grow. In my work with gifted children, I would say that eighty percent who have problems have not been given the right to be themselves by their environment and have experienced a lack of respect and understanding because they do not fit into the accepted societal norms.

The problem of fitting in with norms is particularly acute for gifted children. We educate children to want to be the best, to climb the ladder to the top, rather than be themselves. In fact, we are involved in a give-and-take exchange of emotions and actions throughout our lives. Gifted children need to be appreciated for who they are, not what they do, and they need to be given opportunities to appreciate and support others. The objective of both home and school should be to move them toward self-actualization.

In the interdependent model, the concept of self-actualization is essential. Only a self-actualized person can really cope with interdependence in a constructive manner. Otherwise the experience of deficit, personal needs, hunger for recognition, and hunger for inner safety through outer support overshadow our ability to consciously participate in the human network of interdependence. We become blinded to deeds and realities beyond ourselves. On the other hand, we also need the support, help, loving understanding, and mercy of others in order to reach a state of self-actualization. Therefore, the self cannot develop unless the reality of the connections with everything around it is part of this development. This in itself is an example of the reality of interdependence. The self depends on the human and natural environments in order to grow, and the environment depends on the self to treat it with care.

Each person is an influential part of society and of the world. We are both a unit unto ourselves and a part of many larger entities. Each is part of the past, the present, the future. Within an interdependent network, this awareness, this focus on the connectedness with all others, can help us overcome some of our innate loneliness and separateness and thereby give different meaning to our lives.

Education

A focus on interdependence makes a practical impact in many ways on our lives and on the educational process.

- First, it requires changes of habit and focus within ourselves. Only when adults integrate the fact of interdependence into their consciousness can they teach it or model it to children.

- Second, interdependence means that the structure of education should be based on community rather than institutions so children can learn the facts of interdependence through living them. It requires different administrative structures that allow for participation in decision-making by those who are affected by the decisions. We need to allow everyone—whether they are children, teachers, or support workers—the right to a task, a stake, and a voice within the school community.

- Third, the process of education changes. The focus on interdependence can exist in school groups by stressing cooperation rather than competition, by offering cooperative activities as well as cooperative play equipment, and by solving conflicts within this context through discussion groups and other problem-solving activities.

While traditional education stresses skill learning, in the interdependent model concept learning is greatly emphasized. The curriculum from preschool on can reflect this focus. Geography, social studies, and science can and should be offered at an early age with emphasis on interdependence, on the likenesses and differences among peoples all over the world and their relationships to one another. Global and ethical considerations thus become part of all subject matter.

The concept of values-free education is counter to that of interdependence. Information and knowledge learned in these learning situations are usually used to support the competitive, hierarchical success model.

178 SELECTED WRITINGS AND SPEECHES

Values-free education avoids addressing the ethical questions of our times, which surround us everywhere, and does not give children the tools to cope with or become involved with them as they grow older. These questions range from how to use atomic energy to whether or not to keep terminally ill patients alive, as well as our responsibility to abolish world hunger and to preserve our environment. All children, but especially gifted children, are most interested in such questions and will voluntarily ask them. They can be discussed with increasing complexity, beginning with very young children.

The Gifted

I have not related my ideas about empathy and ethics only to gifted children because I believe that these thoughts are universally applicable and not limited to the gifted. However, they are of specific importance for the gifted and are particularly appropriate to the unique characteristics of this group.

The gifted are global thinkers and are apt to see the whole before they concern themselves with the details. The gifted are complex thinkers and are better able than others to discern the intricacies of interdependence. They are concept-oriented and have an enormous desire to make sense of this world, to master it, and to make an impact on it. They are also research-minded—they want to find out because of their inner need for intellectual and emotional order. They are interested in the past and are very concerned with the future.

All of these characteristics lead them toward the concept of interdependence. It is now up to us to open the door for them and help them make sense of these concepts. The gifted are our hope for the future. They are our hope for the discovery and development of the laws of interdependence, which will enable them to lead this world toward a better future.

Global Awareness and the Young Child

Delivered at the "Sharing the Leadership" conference held at the Roeper City and Country School in Bloomfield Hills, Michigan (November, 1991).

We need to create an environment that strives to preserve the uniqueness of young children and simultaneously integrate them into the large global entity, just as the heart is a distinct organ within the body.

Global awareness, in my understanding, is not a geographical term but an attitude, a mindset, a way of seeing ourselves as an integral part of every aspect of the globe. It is a conscious realization that we are totally intertwined and interdependent with all things on earth because we are not really separate from them. Motivated by an earnest desire to develop an understanding of global interdependence, people often ask me how they can help their young children to develop a sense of global awareness. The real question that needs to be asked, however, is how we can keep young children from losing their inborn sense of global awareness and of being supported by a protective world of which they are a part. Young children and newborns are not yet separate from the world. Their energy, their drive to learn and grow, exists within the context of a family and a community. As young children grow, they unfold like flowers rooted in the soil of life.

The task in the case of young children, therefore, is how to create an environment that will keep them from developing a feeling of being on the outside and separated from their world, from feeling excluded rather than included. We need to create an environment that strives to preserve the uniqueness of young children and simultaneously integrate them into the large global entity, just as the heart is a distinct organ within the body.

I believe that society's attitudes and the reality of the educational process separate children from their world. The traditional education, which begins at birth, is a process that leads to personal success, learning

179

how to win the competition. This means that individuals are pitted against each other. Individuals, teams, or nations can win only if the opponent loses. This attitude denies the fact that we are interdependent and focuses on the qualitative differences between people. Ironically, the greatest interdependence exists between enemies or competitors, for they have to react suspiciously toward each other's every move. Yet there is no greater isolation than this, for they must keep all information strictly apart from each other. Therefore, it is obvious that a competitive society serves to isolate children from the global environment.

Emphasis on cooperation and sharing, on the other hand, means positive participation in the community, integration rather than isolation. A global point of view creates an ever-widening circle of communities within the total global one. Young children are, of course, self-centered. Their selves are the starting point of life awareness. As they grow, the light of experience develops within them a growing awareness. Throughout this development, if not hindered by conditional acceptance, more and more global awareness becomes incorporated into the experience of self. Even the recognition of differences in objects and people becomes part of the interconnected vision of their world.

I am always moved at the empathy and identification with others that young children are capable of feeling and showing. There have been many occasions in my work with preschool children when I watched one child consoling another who was crying over being separated from his mother. The verbally gifted child may explain this to the teacher as follows: "I know how he feels. It was hard for me at first, too. I was afraid that my mother would never come back. Then I learned that she always comes back. I even learned that she thinks of me while she is gone. I think I can make him feel better because I know how it feels."

When children are born, they open their eyes to a strange new world around them, and everything in them strives to become familiar with this world and enlarge their understanding of it so that their selves can grow within a global network of support and empathy. At almost this moment, a kind of decision is made: the environment and the family provide this global network of integration, love, and empathy as the soil for children's growth, or they do not. Within this network of support, children still need to find their place, to understand the demands of human relations, of giving and taking, loss and tragedy. But this will happen only with a background of unconditional acceptance. Do we make children feel accepted unconditionally, or do we convey to them that they will be accepted only if they succeed in terms of the artificial ways of the world that we have constructed? In the latter case, the young human selves face an unending struggle for survival in this world. The initial opportunity for a widening circle of global awareness is replaced by a growing awareness of the self as being outside of the rest of the world. Human beings therefore grow up with the inner task of creating for themselves a place in competition with all others. They struggle to be accepted rather than use their tremendous energies to strive toward growth within the living community of which they are an accepted part by virtue of their existence.

The clear message every child receives from the adult world is this: "In order to survive, you must strive to be a winner and strive toward the goals we have established. We will help you reach these goals provided you accept them as your own. Expressed in simple words, if you want to be rich, you must sell your soul." It is my belief that the desire for the growth of the self, for the unfolding of the inner agenda of the individual, is the most driving force in every human being. In order for this growth to happen, individuals must feel accepted by, integrated in, and supported by their environment. Society has created a situation in which those goals contradict each other. In order to be accepted, the message goes, you must follow outside expectations, not inner needs. And all the while the inner needs are trying to be heard, and they become anguished and express themselves in inappropriate ways. This is especially true for gifted children, whose needs and sense of awareness are so strong and urgent.

How can we make it possible for children to be connected to themselves *and* the world? The first prerequisite for allowing the sense of global awareness to grow in young children is to provide them with an environment in which mentally healthy children can grow up freely. This requires, of course, a sense of global awareness in the adults who surround children. At the beginning of their lives, children are in many ways at the mercy of adults. Not in all ways, however, because through the very fact of their new existence they make an impact on the interdependent environment. Yet children are born into an existing environment. Is it possible to create an environment that will allow both self-growth and global awareness? Or is this just an idealistic hope that cannot be implemented in practice? I believe that it is a realistic goal and that it has many practical consequences. But it requires a basic change in our attitudes, our philosophies, and our educational structures and goals. It also requires that this changed attitude be reflected in our handling of daily life and in our interactions with nature and the peoples of the world.

This means that our first priority must be to allow children the freedom to be themselves within the global framework. Strangely, such children often have more energy for the competitive tasks they choose to pursue than do children whose families have made a competitive vision of life the basis of those children's acceptance. It means that we must examine our own attitudes in light of the growing global awareness and thus become models for our children.

It means that we must examine our educational structures and change them from institutions to communities that reflect global interdependence in their administrative structures. It means that we must actively try to work toward this change. It means that we need to reexamine our existing curricula, priorities, and methods of evaluation in the light of changed attitudes. For example, we might look at our educational institutions and ask whether they are administrated by a hierarchical structure. Can such a structure foster real human equality, respect, integration, and active participation in the community by each member? Can it teach the realities of community and global interaction? Is the decision-making structure appropriate to an interdependent world? Does skill learning have priority over concept learning, which children need and desire to emotionally integrate and intellectually understand the world? Do adults and children learn methods of conflict resolution through it? Do we expect obedience to authority, or do we try to develop a sense of inner responsibility? These are just a few of the questions that we might begin to ask to bring about big, necessary changes in our attitudes and actions with regard to the many problems that confront us today.

Global awareness is not a new subject to be taught, but a different way of life. Only if we bring about this change in attitude will we save our earth and create the safe world our children are entitled to inherit, and only then will we raise truly healthy children.

The Global Perspective

Published in *The Roeper Review* 13 (1991), pp. 225–226.

> *Indeed, believing that the end justifies the means ignores the fact that the means have a life of their own and carry a powerful message. The process which leads to the attainment of a goal may have a greater impact than the goal itself.... If we use violence to solve a problem, then we establish violence as a legitimate means for conflict resolution which may be applied on future occasions—making violence acceptable to be used by everyone, not only by those in power.*

As I look back from my vantage point of 70 years of living, observing, and interacting, I see before me a huge ocean of humanity. This ocean differs from the rolling seas I love to watch, for it consists of wavelets flailing about, bumping noisily into one another, receding, striking out in another direction, joining forces with other wavelets, separating, combining with wavelets previously attacked, and constantly interfering with each other without a discernible pattern.

Reflecting this same randomness, the disoriented sea of humanity persisted since the beginnings of history as humankind increasingly lost its connection with the ocean of life, the universal ecosystem. As a result, individuals, groups, and nations developed and functioned without unifying guidelines. All focus narrowly on their own goals, aware of the presence of others only to the extent to which those others may interfere with the pursuit of their own needs and desires. On the other hand, I also see areas in which the oneness of the human oceans is clearly visible.

It seems that life plays itself out between the forces of separateness and connectedness, between cooperation and confrontation. The gifted and the creative have slowly changed the world to the extreme in both directions, so that today we know how to destroy and how to heal better than in any age in history. And it is these abilities, and the impact they have on ourselves and our environment, which lead us to perceive ourselves as the masters and owners of the world and to deny the reality of universal interdependence.

Most of today's human interactions are based on the concept of a hierarchy, and only a minority react in a manner which reflects the concept of universal interdependence. The difference between these two perspectives expresses itself in the way we handle every human issue.

Let us take the symbolic question, "Am I my brother's keeper?," which means, "Do I have the fundamental responsibility to support all my fellow human beings?" The concept of hierarchy promotes one answer: The choice is mine. I may feel morally obligated to certain people, and I have the right to exclude others. In other words, I am my brother's keeper according to whatever limits I choose. The concept of interdependence, on the other hand, leads to a different answer: I have no choice, for I depend upon my brother as much as he depends upon me. If I mistreat my brother, mistreatment will become an accepted behavior, and my own safety is threatened. Every issue in life is resolved on the basis of one of these two attitudes, even though current complex situations do not always permit simple solutions in either direction.

It is increasingly clear that behavior based on the precept of hierarchy or "might makes right" as the guiding principle has not produced positive results. We clearly know more now than ever before, yet due to our behavior, we are less secure in many ways than we were in the past. As a result, for the first time in history, a subtle change is taking place, the importance of which is slowly penetrating our consciousness. We are learning that we don't own the world and that our behavior is destroying it. We see that the world's resources, once thought to be ours forever, are finite. We are destroying the ecosystem because we do not respect the laws of interdependence. We are becoming aware that being our brother's keeper is necessary for our survival. We are discovering that it is within our power to reverse the process we created by changing our own behavior.

We have begun to learn some of the techniques of cooperation in several areas. Our behavior in automotive traffic is one of them. Its rules and regulations, based on a concept of interdependence and mutual expectations, are accepted by most motorists. We must consider the needs and actions of other drivers as equal to our own. We must identify and predict other people's behavior and adapt our actions to those behaviors. We have no choice but to trust total strangers to protect our safety. And all this is based on a complex understanding of mutual behavior and the need for self-preservation.

The same subtle change is taking place in terms of the environment. We are slowly reacting to the fact that we are part of the planet's ecological system; this has encouraged us to create a sense of responsibility for the environment in our children. However, even though we are able to think in terms of interdependence in isolated areas, such as the need for recycling, the meaning of total interdependence in every aspect of our inner and outer lives has not as yet been internalized in our thinking and decision-making.

The concept is particularly difficult to understand in terms of the ecology of human relations. How can we remember that every action on our part creates a multitude of reactions in others, which result again in a multitude of actions by others? The spanked, powerless child may learn obedience for the moment and express the resulting anger when he becomes the powerful adult. Indeed, believing that the end justifies the means ignores the fact that the means have a life of their own and carry a powerful message. The process which leads to the attainment of a goal may have a greater impact than the goal itself. Our Constitution stabilized life in our country, even though democratic procedures do not always lead to the best result. However, if we use violence to solve a problem, then we establish violence as a legitimate means for conflict resolution which may be applied on future occasions—making violence acceptable to be used by everyone, not only by those in power. The use of violence grows out of the perception of hierarchy and absolute power, which has led to the present state of the earth and human relations.

During the span of my life, absolute belief in human progress and a steady improvement in the human condition have changed into feelings of deep instability and fear of total destruction. During the same period, our knowledge and abilities have grown dramatically. This shows that our behavior is determined not by what we know, but by our attitudes, our belief systems. It is, therefore, imperative that we develop new attitudes, new beliefs, new methods of conflict resolution, new structures of decision-making, and new structures of institutions based on the concept of total interdependence.

Only when we learn to internalize this new recognition of reality will there be the possibility of developing an enduring world. This will require a change of many basic concepts which have been taken for granted in the past. The concept of obedience changes into one of trust and responsibility; competition and power are replaced by cooperation and participation in decision-making; and a sense of compassion becomes the major motivator for behavior, assigning a minor role to competition. Self-preservation will be seen as preservation of others as well as self and also preservation of the globe. Complex methods of conflict resolution will be based on clear, mutually accepted behavioral expectations and mutual understanding of the situation. All this will provide a totally different framework for the application of our knowledge and creativity.

Clearly, this requires a total change of world view. We have developed the most sophisticated methods of competition and the ability to cope with the dependent/independent model of hierarchy. Our methods of cooperation, on the other hand, are underdeveloped. How can we focus the eyes of the world on the need to develop these new attitudes? How can we bring about the changes? I believe education is the obvious forum for this necessary development. Only if we adults learn to incorporate the change, and expose children to it at a young age, can we expect people to become accustomed to this new attitude.

This requires a change of emphasis for education. *Instead of attitudes treated as accessories to the acquisition of skills and knowledge, skills should exist within the framework of developing global attitudes.* A new approach to education needs to be developed, one that may provide the solutions the school reform activists are seeking. School reform has been the topic for discussion among educators for some time. Underlying this desire for reform has been the hope that education will solve some of the world's problems. Thus far, we have been disappointed, because no positive results have been achieved. This is because we are looking for solutions by improving old methods, by doing more of the same. What is required is global re-education. What is needed is a common set of attitudes and mutual expectations—a vision shared, developed, and understood by all peoples of the world.

I believe that global re-education is the task and responsibility of the field of education. This responsibility falls especially on educators of the gifted, who can encourage the gifted to use their special abilities to invent interdependent approaches to solving world problems. I would like, therefore, to challenge all educators to take on the task of making an impact on the future of the world. Let us reverse our present course and replace deep concern with new hope for the future.

Education as the Agent for Fundamental Change

Unpublished article (1991).

Education must lead the way.

We live amidst an explosion of knowledge and an implosion of wisdom. There is a general consensus that things are not going well in this world, that we are not managing our affairs well, that we have exploited the earth and, if there is not a basic change, our world is in mortal danger.

It is clear that the major problem on earth can be attributed to the behavior of people. Our behavior is governed by our attitudes. Our attitudes result from our perceptions of the world and from our basic needs.

We have erred in our view of the world in fundamental ways. Also, we have made education and, hence, our knowledge and information the handmaidens of these misperceptions. Education is perpetuating the errors, namely:

- A misinterpretation of the basis on which our world and the universe exist and function.

- A misinterpretation of the essence of the individual living human being.

How Have We Misinterpreted?

The most outstanding feature of our reality is the inescapable, total interdependence of all things on earth, animate and inanimate. Even though we cannot escape the reality of this fact, our thoughts and emotions are not truly grasping it. Too long have we built a tradition based on opposing concepts, those of the dependency of the many and the independence of the few, powerful and powerless. Furthermore, we have disrupted the ecology and exploited nature, believing we were its masters.

187

Our manner of appropriating, consuming, and wasting "resources" is tearing apart the fabric that sustains life on the planet.

We have not understood that all living things and, hence, all human beings are defined by who they feel themselves to be and not by what they do. The necessity to fulfill the needs of the "I," of the innermost being, is conscious and unconscious motivation for all of our actions. Only when an inner satisfaction is achieved can we begin truly to understand the miracle of interdependence, for it is also the miracle of our connectedness with each other.

What Consequences Must We Draw from These Insights?

* We must realize the errors and understand that our survival on the planet requires a deep and fundamental change of attitude.

* This change is absolutely necessary. It is also possible.

* We must have complete emotional and intellectual understanding of the need for change and pursue it with passion.

* To grasp the fact of interdependence must mean that everyone has power and no one is powerless.

* Understanding the interdependence gives us the means and points to the methods for peaceful conflict resolution.

* By competition, we limit everyone's power. By cooperation, we increase it.

* There are no true winners or losers, only apparent and temporary ones.

* There is not one cause-and-effect, but many causes and many effects.

* Each action, each event—past, present, and future—must be interpreted in the light of interdependence.

If we internalize these understandings, all of our wonderful capacity, knowledge, and information will increase peace and harmony in the world, whereas now, the same capacity, knowledge, and information lead to disharmony and destruction.

If our educational reforms are based on these insights, they will be true reforms. Then education can become the education for change, rather than perpetuating the error. Education must lead the way.

Suggestions for Further Reading

Bergen, D. *Play as a Medium for Learning and Development.* Portsmouth, NH: Heineman Educational Books, Inc., 1987.

Brandwein, P.F. *Elements in a Strategy for Teaching Science in the Elementary School.* New York: Harcourt Brace Jovanovich, Inc., 1962.
— *Substance, Structure, and Style in the Teaching of Science.* New York: Harcourt Brace Jovanovich, Inc., 1965.
— *Toward a Discipline of Responsible Consent.* New York: Harcourt Brace and World, Inc., 1969.
— *A Permanent Human Agenda: The Humanities.* Ventura, CA: Office of the Ventura County Superintendent of Schools, 1983.

Bruner, J. S. *The Process of Education.* Cambridge, MA: Harvard University Press, 1960.

Dukas, H., & Hoffman, B. *Albert Einstein: The Human Side.* Princeton, NJ: Princeton University Press, 1979.

Erikson, E.H. *Childhood and Society.* New York: W.W. Norton and Company, 1963. (Original work published in 1950.)

Freud, A. *Normality and Pathology in Childhood: Assessment and Development.* New York: International Universities Press, 1965.

Freud, S. *The Standard Edition of the Complete Psychological Works* (Vols. 1–24, J. Strachey, Ed.). London: Hogarth Press, 1953–1974.

Greenacre, P. *Emotional Growth: Psychoanalytic Study of the Gifted.* New York: International Universities Press, 1971.

Hesse, H. *Beneath the Wheel.* New York: Bantam Books, 1968.

Inhelder, B. *The Early Growth and Logic of the Child.* New York: Harper & Row, 1964.

Kohlberg, I. *Collected Papers on Moral Development and Moral Education.* Blue Book. Cambridge: Moral Education and Research Foundation, 1973.
— *Collected Papers on Moral Development and Moral Education.* Yellow Book. Cambridge: Moral Education and Research Foundation, 1975.

Kohut, H. *The Analysis of the Self.* New York: International Universities Press, 1971.
— *The Restoration of the Self.* Chicago: University of Chicago Press, 1977.

Lewis, B.A. *The Kid's Guide to Social Action.* Minneapolis: Free Spirit Publishing, 1991.

Maier, H. *Three Theories of Child Development.* New York: Harper & Row, 1965.

Miller, A. *Prisoners of Childhood.* New York: Basic Books, Inc., 1981.

Piaget, J. *The Child's Conception of Numbers* (3rd ed.). London: Routledge & Kegan Paul, 1964.
—& Inhelder, B. *The Early Growth of Logic in the Child.* New York: Harper & Row, 1964.

Piechowski, M.M. "Emotional Development and Emotional Giftedness," in N. Colangelo & G.A. Davis (Eds.), *Handbook of Gifted Education.* Boston: Allyn & Bacon, 1991, pp. 285–306.

Poole, L., and Line, L. *Elementary Science for the Gifted: An Open Classroom Approach.* Science and Children series. National Science Teachers' Association, 1979.

Roeper, A. *Educating Children for Life: The Modern Learning Community.* Monroe, NY: Trillium Press, 1990.
— "Focus on Global Awareness." *World Gifted,* 12 (4), Newsletter of the World Council for Gifted and Talented Children, pp. 19–21 (1991).
— "Identifying the Young Gifted Child." *Parents' Press,* 9 (1), 1,4 (1988).
— "Planning for the Gifted: A New Task for Nursery School Educators." *Gifted Child Quarterly* (1983).
— "Some Observations about Gifted Pre-School Children." *Journal of Nursery Education,* 9 (3), (1963).
—& McCloud, M. *Science for Young Children.* Bloomfield Hills, MI: Published by A. Roeper and M. McCloud, © 1965.
—& Roeper, G. *The Philosophy of the Roeper School.* Bloomfield Hills, MI: Published by A. Roeper and G. Roeper, 1981.
—Hooper, F.H., and Sigel, I.E. "A Training Procedure for Acquisition of Piaget's Conservation of Quantity: A Pilot Study and Its Replication." *British Journal of Educational Psychology,* 36 (3), pp. 301–311 (November, 1966).

Silverman, Linda. "The Global Learner." Unpublished speech delivered at the World Conference for Gifted and Talented Children, University of Toronto, Faculty of Education, 371 Bloor Street West, Toronto, Ontario, Canada M5S 2R7.

Wolff, P.H. *The Developmental Psychologies of Jean Piaget and Psychoanalysis.* New York: International Universities Press, 1960.

About the Author

Annemarie Roeper was born in Vienna, Austria, in August, 1918. She grew up in Germany, where she lived in her parents' boarding school. This was a community structured around a philosophy of humanism and Freudian child psychology. When her family had to leave Germany, they emigrated to the U.S. She and her husband, George, founded the Roeper City and Country School in Bloomfield Hills, Michigan. Their strongest motivation was to create an environment which would allow children to grow up with a minimum of hostility, so they would not feel the need to mistreat other human beings, as the German youth of their day had been led to do. They based their educational philosophy on that of Dr. Roeper's parents, expanding it and also changing it as their own experience grew.

The school was founded in 1941. In 1956, it became a school for gifted children. Annemarie Roeper served as head of the lower school until her retirement in 1980. At that time, she and her husband moved to Oakland, California, where he died in 1992. She now directs a consultation service for gifted children and their parents.

Dr. Roeper has authored four books for young gifted children and has been widely published in books and in national and international professional journals and magazines. Her most recent book, *Educating Children for Life: The Modern Learning Community* (Trillium Press, 1990), elaborates a self-actualization interdependence model (SAI). She continues to serve as executive editor of *The Roeper Review,* a journal on gifted education. In the past, she served on numerous local, state, and national committees on gifted education.

Today Dr. Roeper continues to work toward helping parents and educators understand the inner agenda of the child and our obligation to create a livable world.

Index

More Free Spirit Books

What Kids Need to Succeed
Proven, Practical Ways to Raise Good Kids
by Peter L. Benson, Ph.D., Judy Galbraith, M.A.,
and Pamela Espeland

The Survival Guide for Parents of Gifted Kids
How to Understand, Live with, and Stick Up for Your Gifted Child
by Sally Yahnke Walker, M.A.

Bringing Out the Best
A Resource Guide for Parents of Young Gifted Children
by Jacqulyn Saunders, M.Ed., with Pamela Espeland

Teaching Gifted Kids in the Regular Classroom
Strategies and Techniques Every Teacher Can Use to Meet the
Academic Needs of the Gifted and Talented
by Susan Winebrenner, M.A.

Managing the Social and Emotional
Needs of the Gifted
A Teacher's Survival Guide
by Connie C. Schmitz, Ph.D., and Judy Galbraith, M.A.

To place an order, or to request a free copy of Free
Spirit's 1994 Parents' Choice approved catalog of
SELF-HELP FOR KIDS® materials, write or call:

Free Spirit Publishing Inc.
400 First Avenue North, Suite 616
Minneapolis, MN 55401-1730
toll-free (800)735-7323
local (612)338-2068